Praise for *The*

"Each year, a vivid snapshot of what a distinguished poet finds exciting, fresh, and memorable: and over the years, as good a comprehensive overview of contemporary poetry as there can be."
—Robert Pinsky

"*The Best American Poetry* series has become one of the mainstays of the poetry publication world. For each volume, a guest editor is enlisted to cull the collective output of large and small literary journals published that year to select seventy-five of the year's 'best' poems. The guest editor is also asked to write an introduction to the collection, and the anthologies would be indispensable for these essays alone; combined with [David] Lehman's 'state-of-poetry' forewords and the guest editors' introductions, these anthologies seem to capture the zeitgeist of the current attitudes in American poetry."
—Academy of American Poets

"A high volume of poetic greatness . . . in all of these volumes . . . there is brilliance, there is innovation, there are surprises."
—*Publishers Weekly* (starred review)

"A year's worth of the very best!"
—*People*

"A preponderance of intelligent, straightforward poems."
—*Booklist*

"A 'best' anthology that really lives up to its title."
—*Chicago Tribune*

"An essential purchase."
—*The Washington Post*

"For the small community of American poets, *The Best American Poetry* is the *Michelin Guide*, the *Reader's Digest*, and the Prix Goncourt."
—*L'Observateur*

OTHER VOLUMES IN THIS SERIES

THE
BEST
AMERICAN
POETRY
2020

◇ ◇ ◇

Paisley Rekdal, Editor

David Lehman, Series Editor

SCRIBNER POETRY

NEW YORK LONDON TORONTO SYDNEY NEW DELHI

Scribner Poetry
An Imprint of Simon & Schuster, Inc.
1230 Avenue of the Americas
New York, NY 10020

First Scribner edition September 2020

SCRIBNER POETRY and design are registered trademarks of The Gale Group, Inc.,
used under license by Simon & Schuster, Inc., the publisher of this work.

For information about special discounts for bulk purchases,
please contact Simon & Schuster Special Sales at 1-866-506-1949
or business@simonandschuster.com.

The Simon & Schuster Speakers Bureau can bring authors to your live event.
For more information or to book an event, contact the Simon & Schuster Speakers
Bureau at 1-866-248-3049 or visit our website at www.simonspeakers.com.

Manufactured in the United States of America

1   3   5   7   9   10   8   6   4   2

Library of Congress Control Number: 88644281

ISBN 978-1-9821-0659-1
ISBN 978-1-9821-0660-7 (pbk)
ISBN 978-1-9821-0661-4 (ebook)

CONTENTS

David Lehman was born in New York City. Educated at Stuyvesant High School and Columbia University, he spent two years as a Kellett Fellow at Clare College, Cambridge, and worked as Lionel Trilling's research assistant upon his return from England. His books include *One Hundred Autobiographies: A Memoir* (Cornell University Press, 2019), *Playlist: A Poem* (University of Pittsburgh Press, 2019), and *Poems in the Manner Of* (Scribner, 2017). He is the editor of *The Oxford Book of American Poetry* (Oxford, 2006) and *Great American Prose Poems: From Poe to the Present* (Scribner, 2003). *A Fine Romance: Jewish Songwriters, American Songs* (Schocken, 2009) won the Deems Taylor Award from the American Society of Composers, Authors, and Publishers (ASCAP) in 2010. *Sinatra's Century* (HarperCollins) was published in 2015, as was *The State of the Art: A Chronicle of American Poetry, 1988–2014* (Pittsburgh), a gathering of the forewords he had written for the *Best American Poetry* series. A contributing editor of *The American Scholar*, Lehman lives in New York City and in Ithaca, New York.

FOREWORD

by David Lehman

◇   ◇   ◇

To one who monitors the news for manifestations of poetry in unusual places, 2019 did not disappoint. The cover of the March 25 issue of *Time* featured a picture of an orange peach. The headline: "Do They Dare?" The subhead: "The Democrats will likely impeach." The echo of "The Love Song of J. Alfred Prufrock," the prematurely balding fellow who wonders whether he has the gumption to eat a peach, confirmed something I learned teaching a course called "Great Poems" at New York University: that "Prufrock" remains the modern poem they love best, these talented first-year students who qualified for the college's honors program and enjoyed memorizing sonnets, comparing carpe diem poems by Donne and Marvell, and discussing whether "Kubla Khan" was really a mere fragment, as its author claimed.

On the front page of *The Wall Street Journal* bearing the same date, a tripartite headline observing haiku rules caught my eye: "Haikus About Space/Make Science Less Tedious/So Hope Scientists." Daniela Hernandez's story imparted news of "sciku," the use of the haiku form instead of a one-sentence summary of a study in lunar and planetary science. For example, Áine O'Brien's "The Effects of Shock and Raman Laser Irradiation on the Maturity of Organics in Martian Meteorites" is easier to grasp when summarized in seventeen syllables spread over three lines in units of five, seven, and five syllables: *Look at falling sky / Rock from big red rock in black / Sky to find life signs*. That is quite impressive, and the whole phenomenon adds to evidence I have gathered that the haiku may be the perfect form for an age of shortened attention spans.

In 1986, the Library of Congress rechristened the position of "consultant in poetry" to "poet laureate." Since then, the designation has spread from nation to state, city, county, and borough. In April, the Academy of American Poets announced that thirteen poets laureate will receive a combined sum exceeding one million dollars "to support civic programs." One of the lucky thirteen is the guest editor of this year's *Best American Poetry*. Paisley Rekdal, poet laureate of Utah, plans to sponsor a statewide poetry festival and to launch Mapping Literary Utah, a website devoted to the work of writers who live or have lived in Utah. Jeanetta Calhoun Mish, poet laureate of Oklahoma, will present poetry workshops in rural areas. Grace Cavalieri of Maryland is lining up newspapers to publish Maryland poets.

Dana Gioia, in his stint as poet laureate of California, visited each county in the state, a feat requiring heroic measures of stamina. Karen Craigo, Missouri's current poet laureate, plans to gather a collection of poems from all of the state's 114 counties. Claudia Castro Luna, poet laureate of the state of Washington, will convene poetry workshops and readings along the entire length of the Columbia River. William Carlos Williams wrote that he was "the happy genius of [his] household," and maybe that's another way of saying the poet laureate of the backyard. The designation does get taken to an incongruous extreme at times. Last August, *Atlanta* magazine broke the story that Waffle House has tapped Georgia Tech professor Karen Head as the chain's first official poet laureate. When asked how a Waffle House is like a poem, Professor Head pointed out that both poetry and hash browns are "made things."

More news of poetry's therapeutic powers surfaced in 2019. In addition to its palliative value, reading or writing poetry "can heal," according to the poet and physician Rafael Campo, who teaches at Harvard Medical School and works at Beth Israel Deaconess Medical Center in Boston. A pilot study at Northwestern University's medical school aims to ascertain whether "reading poetry with patients has the potential to help alleviate doctor burnout."[1] During the daily "grim half-hour" when the editors of the *New York Times*'s national desk convene, the session begins with a poem, somewhat in the way prayers may have served in the past. The poems come from Billy Collins's anthology *Poetry 180*. Marianne Boruch, Langston Hughes, Wordsworth, David Ignatow, Paul Verlaine, and Charles Simic are among the poets whose words read aloud have blessed the editors.[2] It is nevertheless true that *poetry* still shows up sometimes in the old philistine way. A dour *New*

---

1 Sumathi Reddy, "A Prescription of Poetry to Help Patients Speak Their Minds," in *The Wall Street Journal*, December 1, 2019, p. A11.

2 Marc Lacey, "How Poetry Shakes Up the National Desk's Morning Meetings," *Times Insider*, March 5, 2020.

Yorker article on that most dour of subjects, Brexit, listed some of the woes that have befallen Great Britain since June 2015:

> [Boris] Johnson asked the Queen to shut down Parliament; the Supreme Court opened it up again. He called for a general election; the Labour Party, led by Jeremy Corbyn, refused to agree to one unless Brexit was delayed. The pound fell. Death threats multiplied. Politicians quoted poetry. A third of British adults said that Brexit had affected their mental health. A man in a clown outfit stood outside the gates of Parliament shouting, "Save our bendy bananas!"[3]

In that succession of dire sentences, you wonder what "politicians quoted poetry" is doing.

Walt Whitman and Emily Dickinson are the two nineteenth-century American poets who continue to exert the greatest influence on contemporary poetry. In 2019, the bicentennial of Whitman's birth was celebrated with exhibitions devoted to the poet at the New York Public Library, the Morgan Library, and the Grolier Club in New York City. The shows triggered glowing articles about the bard of democracy. In *The New Yorker*, Peter Schjeldahl made the astute observation that "If Keats was 'half in love with easeful death,' Whitman was head over heels for it, as a subject fit for his titanic drive to coax positive value from absolutely everything."[4] In September, the U.S. Postal Service released its 85-cent Walt Whitman stamp covering mail weighing up to three ounces. The Whitman stamp features a portrait of the poet by Sam Weber based on a photograph taken by Frank Pearsall in 1869. A lilac bush and hermit thrush in the background are meant to remind correspondents of Whitman's elegy for Abraham Lincoln, "When Lilacs Last in the Door-Yard Bloom'd."

The Library of America published *Walt Whitman Speaks: His Final Thoughts on Life, Writing, Spirituality, and the Promise of America* edited by Brenda Wineapple. (In conversation, Whitman foresaw threats to "free speech, free printing, free assembly," amounting to a "weapon of menace to our future.") Also in 2019, poets made efforts to accord land-

3 Sam Knight, "The Long Goodbye," *The New Yorker*, November 4, 2019, p. 18.

4 Peter Schjeldahl, "The Song of a Nation," *The New Yorker*, June 24, 2019, pp. 74–75.

mark status to Whitman's Brooklyn residence at 99 Ryerson Street. Seeing the house for the first time "brought tears to my eyes," Douglas Crase wrote in a plea to the Landmarks Preservation Commission. "Through that door space in 1855 walked Walt Whitman, at the very time he was about to publish the book that would change American literature forever." The landmarks commission has balked because the structure is undistinguished architecturally. Nevertheless it is the only remaining New York City building that served as the poet's residence. There are shrines to the poet in Huntington, Long Island, where he was born, and in Camden, New Jersey, where he spent his final years. But the place where he lived while finishing and publishing *Leaves of Grass* is unmarked and subject to the considerations of realtors and builders. Shouldn't there be a site in Brooklyn to honor the author of "Crossing Brooklyn Ferry"?

At an international festival at the Walt Whitman Birthplace in August, Robert Schultz delivered a talk on "Walt Whitman and the Civil War," reflecting the work he and Binh Danh have done collaboratively on this important subject. *War Memoranda: Photography, Walt Whitman, and Memorials*, their book, contains Danh's cyanotypes of Civil War battlefields and Schultz's poems, prose, and chlorophyll prints of Whitman and of Civil War soldiers developed in the flesh of leaves. The conference at the birthplace was moderated by the redoubtable Ed Folsom of the University of Iowa, who chaired as many as eight conferences devoted to the "good gray poet" in 2019.

In conjunction with *North American Review*, Brian Clements launched "Every Atom" (as in "every atom belonging to me as good belongs to you"), a series of two hundred entries on consecutive days from poets and other Whitman lovers, who were asked to select a passage from Walt and to annotate it, as Martín Espada did on day one (May 31) with reflections on the wonderful lines from "Song of Myself" that begin "Walt Whitman, an American, one of the roughs, a kosmos." It is a happy choice, illustrating "Whitman the visionary, the prophet of the new politics and the new poetics."[5]

On June 11, the poet Richard Jackson quoted these famous lines from "Song of Myself": "Do I contradict myself? / Very well, then . . . I contradict myself. / I am large . . . I contain multitudes." The lines are

---

5 Espada quotes the passage as it appeared in the 1855 edition of the poem. Whitman weakened the line in later versions: "Walt Whitman, a Kosmos, of Manhattan the son."

Whitman's way of saying, with Emerson, that "A foolish consistency is the hobgoblin of little minds, adored by little statesmen and philosophers and divines." There are, Jackson said, dozens of Walt Whitmans afloat. "I was once Walt Whitman," Jorge Luis Borges wrote in "Camden, 1892," and one notes, too, Pessoa's "Salutation to Walt Whitman"; Lorca's "Ode to Walt Whitman" and Neruda's ode with the same title; Hart Crane extending his hand to his forerunner in "The Bridge"; Allen Ginsberg imagining Whitman in a California supermarket, and A. R. Ammons beholding the "radiance" of creation in "The City Limits."

The lines justifying self-contradiction can amount to an anticipatory defense of personae, masks, and heteronyms. On June 22, Julia Alvarez (whose work is included in this year's *Best American Poetry*) picked up the theme, writing that "In his 'Oda a Walt Whitman,' Neruda claims Whitman taught him to be Americano by celebrating a hemispheric America large enough to include everybody. There was something simpatico—a word Whitman himself uses—between the poet and Hispanic ways of seeing and saying and moving through the world. In fact, when I encountered Jorge Luis Borges's translation of *Leaves of Grass* into Spanish (*Hojas de Hierba*), the poem didn't sound translated—it flowed beautifully in Spanish, as if that had been its origin language."

The celebration of Whitman's bicentennial was complicated by the knowledge that in 1874 Walt denigrated the intellect of black people. Matthew Zapruder in his "Poem for Harm" spoke of his disappointment: "I believed you / your whole life you made // one book some people / now take out into the forest // to ritually burn / because elsewhere you wrote // when you were more than / old enough to know // what you truly thought / of the intellect // of black folks who / were not inside your song."[6] Even as we enshrine Whitman, it is wise to remember that approval of his poetry was never universal—that as he aged, he tended to revise his poems for the worse and that biographical facts or rumors injurious to his reputation surface now and then. Poetry has always been a contested field, and Willa Cather, back in 1896, argued that Whitman's egalitarianism meant the forfeiture of a moral imagination. She wrote that he "accepted the world just as it is and glorified it, the seemly and unseemly, the good and the bad. He had no conception of a difference in people or in things. All men had bodies and were alike to him, one about as good as another. To live was to fulfill

6 Matthew Zapruder, *Father's Day* (Copper Canyon Press, 2019).

all natural laws and impulses. To be comfortable was to be happy. To be happy was the ultimatum. He did not realize the existence of a conscience or a responsibility. He had no more thought of good or evil than the folks in Kipling's Jungle book."

Maybe so, but I would prefer to let Neruda, as translated by Martín Espada, have the last word. Here is the conclusion of "Ode to Walt Whitman":

But
your voice
sings
in the train stations
on the edge of town,
your words
splash
like
dark water
across
the
loading docks
at night,
and your people,
white
and black,
poor
people,
simple
as all people
are simple,
do not forget
your bell:
they congregate singing
beneath
the magnitude
of your spacious life:
they walk among people
with your love
nurturing the pure evolution
of *fraternidad* across the earth.

★　★　★

I have a natural respect for poets who write prose, can meet deadlines, and undertake ambitious projects. Paisley Rekdal does these things energetically. For her poems she has won the admiration of other estimable poets; her work was selected for five of the last eight volumes of *The Best American Poetry*. Among her books I have a special fondness for *Intimate: An American Family Photo Album*, a memoir dealing with the mixed-race marriage of her parents. The prose is interspersed with the photos of Edward Curtis, who, in Theodore Roosevelt's words, "lived on intimate terms with many different tribes of the mountains and plains." Some of Rekdal's entries are prose poems. One begins: "As a child I was often confused as to who was Chinese and who was white. I thought David Carradine was Chinese. I thought Yul Brynner was Chinese. I thought Tom Brokaw, who looked like my mother's youngest brother, Kingsley, was Chinese. Everyone was potentially Chinese, just as everyone was also potentially white." Paisley worked hard on this volume, never losing her sense of humor. On January 13, she told her Twitter followers. "In the unending series of online distractions to help keep me from finishing this introductory essay to a volume of poetry I edited, I have bought a 2-piece satin suit, an owl house, pendant lights, an ice cream cake, slippers, and now a ukulele." One list of her favorite poems from the year's magazines was headed "Poems I will not cut on pain of death."

At a time when misinformation can spread with internet speed, it bears repeating that the choices for each volume in *The Best American Poetry* series are made by the guest editor, whose autonomy is guaranteed; the series editor can advise but not insist. Aside from picking the guest editor and assisting her, the series editor attends mainly to the preparation, production, and promotion of the book. It is his job to supervise the process—to write a foreword, to obtain and to edit the guest editor's introduction and the contributors' notes and comments, to enforce such rules as we have (no translations, for example), to acquire permissions, to assemble the manuscript, to help choose the cover art, and to work with the publisher as we rush to meet imminent deadlines.

The Best American Poetry is constantly evolving not just because of the passage of time—the 2020 volume will necessarily differ from the one dated 1990—but because there is a different guest editor each year. Like a moving object in space, poetry cannot be located with precision because the tools of measurement affect the outcome. The best we can do is to represent as many legitimate points of view as are commensurate with the size of the nation, the various factions competing for attention, the demographic and regional diversity of our writers, and the rival conceptions of poetic excellence. I may or may not agree with the guest editor's selections, but the whole point of the exercise is to foreground that person's taste, to allow a practitioner of the art to win a readership for the poems that she or he admires the most. This is so whether the criteria are based on personal taste, a political conviction, a sense of some ineffable something that resists definition, a value placed on intelligence, urgency, charm, complexity, emotional resonance, the pleasure principle, or principles derived from Arnold, Eliot, Leavis, Ricks, Bloom, Vendler, or one's friends at the AWP convention. Each year's volume may be consulted as a criticism of last year's. No volume is absolutely definitive. A friend once quipped that people love to argue about an anthology; some put it down, but everyone wants to be in it. The effect is magnified by social media.

In her introduction to this year's volume, the guest editor revives the venerable tradition of querying the title of the anthology. Back in 1988, John Ashbery anticipated the "best" problem and joked, "Maybe we should call the book 'OK Poems of the Year.'" I often wonder why poets have worried the question while it goes unmentioned in anthologies of the year's best stories and essays. If anyone has a theory, I'd like to hear it. In his introduction to *The Best American Poetry 2006*, Billy Collins sizes it up this way: "Several past guest editors have felt a need to make apologies for that superlative. In these hypersensitive times when the lighting of a cigarette is regarded as a mortal offense, why be surprised that the notion of ranking poems would be cause for discomfort?"

★ ★ ★

In 1998, we published a volume entitled *The Best of the Best American Poetry: 1988–1997* with selections from the first ten years of the series. The choices were made by Harold Bloom, the Yale University eminence who died last fall at age eighty-nine. Bloom was the most famous, most prolific, and most influential literary critic in America from the time he published *The Anxiety of Influence* in 1973. The title of that book has entered our critical vocabulary, as has Bloom's thesis that a "strong" poet must overcome the influence of a powerful precursor. To become himself, Wordsworth had to contend with Milton, for example, while John Ashbery had to endure a wrestling match with Wallace Stevens.

I had met Harold quite by chance six years earlier. In September

1967, as I was about to enter my sophomore year at Columbia, I borrowed my parents' car and, knowing that Yale began its semester a few weeks before we did, drove to New Haven with a friend hoping to sit in on a class. The administrator we approached was kind enough to direct us to a seminar in modern poetry taught by Harold Bloom. It was the first day of the semester, and the professor told the group that only four modern poets were worthy of our attention: William Butler Yeats, D. H. Lawrence, Wallace Stevens, and Hart Crane. This was bold. Everyone else was taking notes, and Bloom glowered and asked me why I wasn't doing so. Instead of answering I asked what happened to Eliot, Ezra Pound, William Carlos Williams, and Marianne Moore? "They're not central," he said, which was indisputably a maverick position.

In the 1980s, Bloom embarked on the effort of editing hundreds of volumes of critical essays, turning out an introduction for each. "Harold can write an introduction faster than our staffers can turn out jacket copy," Patricia Baldwin, his chief of staff, told me when I visited New Haven in July 1986. At the time, I was writing regularly for *Newsweek*. At *Time* or *Newsweek* in the good old pre-Net days, the hardest thing about writing a six-column piece on a professor of literature was to persuade your senior editor that you can appeal to a general readership that was generally indifferent to academic scholarship. Here I had a brainstorm. I went in and told my editor that Bloom was "the Henry Kissinger of literary criticism" and got the green light.

I reported that Bloom looked like Zero Mostel and sounded like a combination of Oscar Wilde and an Old Testament prophet. For one who rejoiced in the ecstatic vision of a favorite poet, he exuded a certain charming air of gloom. He told me he knew by heart every line of poetry he ever read that he liked. "My dear," he said, "what matters in literature in the end is surely the idiosyncratic, the individual, the flavor or the color of a particular human suffering." Insomnia allowed him to read and reread to his heart's content.

When the poet John Hollander dropped by, and the three of us went out to lunch, I wondered who would prove the bigger talker, for both John and Harold were amazing monologists (and, incidentally, lifelong Yankee fans). No contest; Harold could outtalk anyone. I liked his avuncular salutations: there was "Uncle Archie" (Ammons), "Uncle Ashbery," and "the noble Merrill." *Newsweek* ran my piece under the heading "Let a Hundred Blooms Flower" (international edition) and "Yale's Insomniac Genius."

Harold edited *The Best of the Best American Poetry, 1988–1997* with his usual flair—and his usual knack for arousing firestorms of disputation. He included selections from nine of the books but nothing from the 1996 volume, which Adrienne Rich had edited. In his introductory essay, Harold launched an attack on multiculturalism and identity poetry—in which the author's sex, age, ethnic identity, class, and race trump other considerations—and made it plain that Adrienne's sensibility and taste were to blame. When I couldn't persuade Harold to hold his fire, I phoned Adrienne to give her a heads-up. She was very gracious. "Don't worry," she said, indicating that she felt it was "an honor" to be thus assailed by Bloom. The *Boston Review* devoted much of an issue to a discussion of Harold's pronouncements. Most of the writers denounced and dissented in vehement terms. I, who do not set out to court controversy but have learned the publishing value of provocation, was relieved when my publisher informed me that the denunciations had helped sell books.

Bloom's energy never flagged, despite two decades of medical woes that would have arrested a lesser person. Harold wrote right up to the end, by longhand when possible. Writing kept him alive. He wrote books, massive tomes in some cases, on Shakespeare, on the American religion, on Genesis (parts of which, he argued, were written by a woman), and on some of his favorite characters, Hamlet, Lear, Cleopatra, Falstaff, Iago.

My last message to Harold was prompted by a reading of his book on *King Lear*. It was on July 21, 2018. "I am reading your book on Lear," I wrote, "and must reaffirm that you are every inch a genius."

★ ★ ★

I write in self-imposed isolation, belatedly, as this book is well into production. The coronavirus that originated in Wuhan, China, and is spreading with the speed of a medieval plague, has mandated "social distancing," a phrase now commonplace. In Wall Street lingo, we have suffered a fearful "black swan event" that no economic model could have forecast. The shock to our systems of living and of thought has not yet been fully absorbed, but already the stock market has tumbled, main streets look like ghost streets, schools are closed, colleges have sent their students home, the NBA has shut down, the NCAA's March Madness was canceled, and Major League Baseball's spring training, too. Even politicians have taken notice. Emergency measures are taking effect. The effort to create an effective vaccine is under way. We can hope that an antidote is in a chemist's test tube even now. Medical scientists are doing their best to "flatten the infection curve"—to limit the spread of this ultra-contagious virus that has already killed many thousands of people and caused whole nations to close down.

Confined to quarters, I have the luxury of thinking about this plague in relation to those in our literature and history—the ten plagues God visited upon the Egyptians in Exodus; the plague Oedipus brought on Thebes when he committed the twin sins of parricide and incest; the bubonic plague that decimated Europe in the fourteenth century. It is possible to regard the current situation allegorically as a punishment we have brought upon ourselves or possibly as a prophecy of geopolitical warfare or a radical solution to the problem Malthus posed. It is also a failure of the imagination inasmuch as we were as unprepared for it as we were at Pearl Harbor on December 7, 1941. The reassuring thing is that we did win the war that we entered on that day.

In the aftermath of the terrorist attack of September 11, 2001, W. H. Auden's "September 1, 1939" gained a new currency. The most famous line of that poem—"We must love one another or die"—was brutalized in an opinion piece in today's *New York Times* (March 19, 2020), which substituted "help" (and "assist") for "love." The more important point is that Auden's poetry endures. Poetry matters. People instinctively turn to poetry during a crisis, for it is then that we become most acutely aware of our need for beauty, truth, wisdom, charm, and delight. American poets are and will be living through a crisis worse than any in my lifetime, and how they respond to it will prove a fascinating test, challenge, and spur.

Paisley Rekdal was born in Seattle and educated at the University of Washington, the University of Toronto Centre for Medieval Studies, and the University of Michigan. She is the author of six books of poetry: *A Crash of Rhinos* (University of Georgia Press, 2000); *Six Girls Without Pants* (Eastern Washington University Press, 2002); *The Invention of the Kaleidoscope* (University of Pittsburgh Press, 2007); *Animal Eye* (Pittsburgh, 2012); *Imaginary Vessels* (Copper Canyon Press, 2016); and *Nightingale* (Copper Canyon, 2019). She has also written four collections of nonfiction: *The Night My Mother Met Bruce Lee* (Pantheon, 2000); *Intimate* (Tupelo Press, 2012); *The Broken Country: On Trauma, a Crime, and the Continuing Legacy of Vietnam* (University of Georgia Press, 2017); and *Appropriate: A Provocation* (W. W. Norton, 2021). She has received a Guggenheim Fellowship, the Amy Lowell Poetry Traveling Fellowship, a Fulbright Fellowship, the Rilke Prize, a National Endowment for the Arts Fellowship, *Narrative*'s Poetry Prize, and the AWP Creative Nonfiction Prize. Her work has appeared in multiple volumes of *The Best American Poetry* series. She teaches at the University of Utah, where she is the creator and editor of the community web project Mapping Salt Lake City. In May 2017, she was named Utah's Poet Laureate and received a 2019 Academy of American Poets' Poets Laureate Fellowship.

INTRODUCTION

by Paisley Rekdal

◇ ◇ ◇

I have the distinct honor of being perhaps the only guest editor of this series at a time when the future of American poetry, at least, isn't dire. According to the National Endowment for the Arts, poetry readership is at an astonishing fifteen-year high: 12 percent of the adult U.S. population, around twenty-eight million people, now say they read poetry. It's gratifying news, made more so by the fact that these readers live in both rural and urban areas. That they are (according to the NEA) mostly female, young, and nonwhite is something that should come as no surprise to anyone who has coached a high school Poetry Out Loud session, or has been cheering on the meteoric rise of poets of color.[1]

And yet with so much good news about poetry, I've been bemused by some of the critical response to it. Of course, the NEA reveals patterns of consumption, not what books readers enjoy, or how they've found them, and certainly not what these readers consider the activity of reading poetry to be. Are readers attending to whole collections, as some of my colleagues wonder, or simply a poem or two that drifts across a feed? Both are acts of reading, but they are not necessarily acts of equal attention. And if this rise in poetry readership is linked to the widespread use of social media, as certain colleagues speculate, perhaps the bump might be most efficiently explained by the presence of Rupi Kaur, the Instagram sensation who has sold three million copies of her books. It is the particular connection between social media, internet hype, and aesthetic consumerism that has led some to dismiss this new readership, grumbling their suspicions (ironically, also on social media) that what passes for poetry on Instagram isn't challenging enough to be considered "good," and barely makes a claim to be poetry. For them, a certain type of audience enjoyment is to be treated with suspicion, if not disdain.

1 https://www.arts.gov/art-works/2018/taking-note-poetry-reading-federal -survey-results.

But, really, how much does it matter how we read poetry? Isn't the point simply to engage with poems, regardless of how they're shared or experienced, leaving aside questions of literary taste? For what reason should we resist the idea that the mark of a good poem is that it simply *means something* to a reader?

It is true that the enjoyment of any art is finally a subjective pleasure, and it is also true that "enjoyment" is not a uniform experience. I once wept myself to hiccups while watching *Hachi: A Dog's Tale* on the Hallmark Channel at 3 AM in a hotel, an experience that drained me so thoroughly I then spent $200 on Cindy Crawford eye creams hawked on the post-film infomercial while recovering. I can watch *Moonlight* or *Taxi Driver*, then turn around and binge *The Real Housewives of New York*; I've felt deep joy among the poems of Emily Dickinson and Terrance Hayes, but also childishly thrilled to the limericks of Swinburne and the doggerel of Ogden Nash. My point is that my enjoyment of one type of writing does not limit my more profound appreciation for another, and that "good" (and certainly "best") is often determined by moment-to-moment needs. In fact, it is my very appreciation for what some might consider "low" entertainment that makes my passion for George Eliot and Charlie Parker and Samuel Taylor Coleridge all the more poignant to me.

I begin my introduction with these questions about pleasure, because, to some extent, they undergird each of my anxieties concerning the words "best," "American," and "poetry." Is consuming more poetry, whether online or in anthologies like these, a "best" development in American reading habits? Is caring about the fact we read poetry, or caring about the kind and type of poetry we *should* be reading, somehow a mark of our culture's fascination with the practice of spiritual self-improvement, and thus a trend that's quintessentially "American"? And what, as our devices stifle concentration, blunt our syntax, and burlesque our sympathies, might we now consider the definition of "poetry" to be?

But I wonder, too, if my anxieties around "Best American Poetry" stem less from how I might define each word than from how I'm meant, as both a poet and a reader, to place poetry on a very precarious pedestal. Poems, it seems, appear to have done everything: they have transcribed and resisted (even if they have not occasioned or ended) revolution, fascism, and war; they have attended births and deaths, marriages and divorces; they elegize and they celebrate; they lambast and they praise; they have shaped the language of both our public and our private lives. They have forced no particular activity upon us, and in that regard they achieve nothing; nevertheless we return to the rhythms and sounds of poetry for our most affecting tragedies and triumphs. They are not foundational to the making of our souls, and yet we insist that without their presence in our culture, without our ability to read and attend to them, our souls are impoverished. Poems are made of words and thus can activate nothing without a reader's consent, and yet we assign to them all the power, authority, and superstition of magic spells. What is a poem, ultimately, but the reader's fantasy of her own humanity?

And yet poems, too, become, in classrooms and in bookstores and in anthologies like this one, flags of cultural ownership. Poetry contains within it a myriad of voices and histories, but the history of American poetry has not always broadcast its inclusion of these voices. Who has "best" tended to overlook and why? What aesthetics do we like to grant that title, and have they always been ones with, if not the widest media exposure, certainly some popular appeal?

But if I think "best" is, finally, a loaded term of cultural convenience, do I then dismiss the possibility of *any* objective evaluation of poetry? Are our definitions of what constitutes excellence to be so hamstrung by our identities and unconscious prejudices that we're now unable or unwilling to critically assess each other's work? Conversely, if "best" is only a political designation, can't I then use this anthology to show you an America and a poetry I want you to see? In which case, in which ways is it culturally "best" of this series to choose me as its editor: the first person of Asian descent since this anthology's inception in 1988?

These questions did not inform the spirit with which I began, and ended, my editorship. Back in the barely memorable blur of late 2018, I approached this volume the way anyone might when presented the opportunity to select for American readers some sense of what the poets were thinking and writing about during 2019, which is to say I began my editorship with fantasies of judicious tastemaking and relevance. I thought about canonicity, and I thought about rigor and talent and required classroom reading, and I thought about all the readers out there languishing in some impoverished airport bookstore, perhaps, wondering what the poets in America were getting up to. And I thought about the poets coming up now in the world who might want to be in such an anthology (because regardless of our dissembling on the matter, poets care very much about being included in this anthology), and then I began to remember my own experience with this series that began more than twenty years ago, when I was in graduate school and *The Best American Poetry* was being taught by one of my workshop professors. At first, I thought it was a subtle challenge—*Here is an anthology in which, if you work very hard, one day you might find yourself validated as a poet*, I thought she was telling us, a thought that both energized and depressed me at the time, though I realize now this was simply her way of offering us, her students, some sense of a poetry landscape that was both wider and aesthetically more diverse than a few select collections could be. What she was offering us, I see now, was an opportunity to find others out there like us. If certain critics today would sneer at how readers call pecking at the poems in their feeds "reading," our own intense gleaning of these anthologies that we did as young poets in the nineties wasn't much different. We were looking for fellowship. We were looking to find ourselves.

In the end, however, I gave up all pretense to posterity. I cannot fake interest in a poem for the sake of producing an anthology meant only for classroom consumption or hierarchical anxieties. After months of reading I was forced to think of this anthology less as a public testament than a private concern. I picked poems for my pleasure and so put nothing automatically aside. If you were a friend, colleague, or former student, if you were frenemy or ex or both, I read you. I wanted to be delighted, and I wanted to find that delight wherever I could. My reading was intense and wide—twenty-five or thirty-five print journals a month, as well as all the online literary journals and daily poetry publishing services such as Verse Daily, Poetry Daily, and the Academy of American Poets' Poem-a-Day series. David Lehman sent regular packets stuffed with notes. Still, my reading couldn't possibly be complete. There are high school and college undergraduate literary journals, there are prison journals, there are community papers and regional and national magazines, there are Instagram feeds and blogs and zines and newsletters. Prior to the internet, an editor of this series might reasonably claim to have read around 70 percent of all poetry published in nationally recognized journals; now, an editor could barely claim to have read 30 percent. Whether or not this is, as some have declared, another Golden Age of Poetry, one thing is for certain: it is the Golden Age of Poetry Publishing, and the result is that a devoted editor could read a brand-new poem published per hour, if she wishes. Possibly per minute.

And on the topic of publishing, I must point out that this anthology—though it includes only mine and David Lehman's names on the cover—is in reality a multiply-authored creation. I am merely the last in a long series of readers that have been working to assemble this particular group of poets for your reading interest. It didn't take long for me to chart the sometimes stark difference in journal editors' tastes, tastes that I began not only to rely upon but to become enamored with. I learned that an excellent editor not only shapes the theme of a single issue, but in turn can shape how individual poems will be read within that journal's pages. In a few cases, I was shocked to see how the resonance of a poem lessened when taken out of the context of the journal itself; the ideal magazine, I soon discovered, helps poems speak to the other poems that surround it, as well as to the included prose pieces. In a few notable cases, I struggled to limit myself to five or fewer excellent poems from a single journal. I even asked David whether the rules could be bent, whether another three or five more names might be added. The answer, sadly, was no. So I want to salute the journals that made my decision-making so arduous, in the hopes that, if nothing else, readers of this anthology might go on to subscribe to them. Kudos in particular to the curatorial work behind *New England Review*, *Kenyon Review*, *Michigan Quarterly Review*, *Waxwing*, and *Tin House*, whose print journal has sadly been shuttered.

In the end, this is a book with a complex, some might say contradictory, aim and readership. Even my own stated objective—pleasure—is an obviously inadequate term to describe the practice of active reading, and the ways that reading itself changes over time. "Pleasure" suggests a state of psychic ease and comfort. But I take pleasure in a variety of poems, just as I take pleasure in a variety of activities over the course of a year, and very few of them offer much easy comfort. I want to think, I want to cry, I want to argue, I want to shout for joy, I want to laugh, I want to be consoled, I want to be challenged, I want to see my world, somehow, both reflected and changed in language. With that last desire in mind, I even began to wonder how much my idea of pleasure in poetry now coincided with my sense of what's been happening in America. This in turn made me revisit previous introductions to this series, where I found this intriguing paragraph:

> Contempt for language, the evisceration of meaning from words, are cultural signs that should not surprise us. Material profit finally has no use for other values, in fact reaps benefits from social incoherence and atomization, and from the erosion of human bonds of trust—in language or anything else. And so

rapid has been the coming-apart during the years . . . in which these poems were being written, so stunned are so many at the violence of the dismantling (of laws, protections, opportunities, due process, mere civilities) that some of us easily forget how the history of this Republic has been a double history, of selective and unequal arrangements regarding property, human bodies, opportunity, due process, freedom of expression, civility and much else.

This is from the introduction Adrienne Rich wrote for *The Best American Poetry 1996*, and it is both heartening and demoralizing to realize how apropos these words might be for today. Heartening, because I can see we have survived these conditions, demoralizing because we must continue to survive them, and worse. If I'd wanted, I could have packed this anthology with poems solely about climate change. Or about the jailing of migrants, police brutality, gun violence, lost reproductive rights, racial microaggressions, "fake news," voter suppression, #MeToo sexual violence, and the havoc of late-stage capitalism. To be sure, there are such poems in this volume. If you are in some airport bookstore right now wondering what the poets in America are getting up to, they are getting up to collectively losing their minds.

All of which has made me wonder whether the particular form of "Americanness" on display in the journals now being published was one of perpetual unease, an endless interrogation of the national values that have betrayed many of its citizens. Perhaps, then, the most consistently "American" trait of our poets is this ability and need to pit the language of poetry against the rhetoric of obfuscation, of disenfranchisement, of division. Over the years, we've watched politicians chip away at words, insisting that relativism, the growth of stock markets, and personal comfort be the yardsticks that determine truth. We've watched scientists hedge about climate change in data and euphemisms the public couldn't parse; we've witnessed public intellectuals pandering to group-think, cowering before the lucubrations of social media. Prior to this last administration, I trusted that good readers would be able to winnow out the wheat from the chaff, but with twenty-four-hour news cycles and the ever-widening maw of the internet, we now seem to be drowning in chaff that powerful institutions, tastemakers, and algorithms insist we accept as gold.

But the problems of language are perpetual: so long as we rely upon words to express ourselves, someone will co-opt them, and perhaps in a nation that fundamentally defines itself through a commitment to free speech, this obsession with words has been and will always be acute. Is this why we have, and need, anthologies like this one? Is this the consolation that poetry best offers us, not only the language in which to examine the piercing realities of our moment in time, but the belief that we can recover from the traumas of our own time; that—if someone else has found imagery adequate to depict her experience for us—certainly we can find a way to words that will translate our realities to others?

I wrote the full draft of this introductory essay in my office in early January 2019, but I finished the copyedited version at home in April 2020. You know what happened in the interim. Because I am a state poet laureate, my inbox was daily stuffed with requests from poetry chain mails and journalists and school administrators and arts program newsletters asking me to supply them with poems, preferably ones that could offer people inspiration. Poetry, it seemed, was the art form of crisis, and as I am a poet it was now my civic duty to offer hope up by the buckets. But I didn't want to read poetry initially; I wanted to lie on the floor and eat everything in sight. It felt traitorous to admit that I myself could barely form a sentence, or that I didn't feel poetry *should* be hopeful, not just because inspiration wasn't why I turned to poetry as a teenager, but because why should I trust a poem that insisted everything, and everyone, would be all right? In my local grocery store, I watched a woman break down shrieking in an empty cleaning products aisle. I watched friends' businesses evaporate overnight. I called my eighty-year-old father daily to beg him to stop walking to the gas station for beer. Alone at my once busy dog park, I listened to a man tap drumsticks along the rim of an inverted brass kettle he'd repurposed, its bowl filling the air with a sound like falling water. Beside him lay a basket stuffed with rolls of toilet paper, candy bars, and packages of Kleenex with a sign tucked inside reading: *Take some. We will weather this together.*

Strangers on trails I ran turned their backs to me and covered their faces when I passed; I did the same to others in turn. An earthquake struck, which triggered over the next month more than a thousand aftershocks. I heard the cries of Cooper's hawks in my trees, and the drifting conversation of couples passing by my window as they walked together each night. Homeless people built tent cities in the park. A Chinese American friend was spat at outside a store. More aftershocks cracked the neighbor's foundation. I bought a two-person survivalist backpack that contained enough freeze-dried food and purified water packets for a week and hid it in my car. I spent days on the computer cheerfully trying to corral students—many who looked drained and ill—into completing pedagogically suspect tasks. I finished every book deadline I'd agreed to in a timely manner and then went to sleep for fifteen hours. What comfort did I think poetry was supposed to offer?

I have never treated poetry as a therapeutic activity; I doubt any serious poet does. And yet if I resist the impulse to turn to poetry for solace, I also risk missing the intimacy that poetry offers us, an intimacy that suggests the author knows my private thoughts and feelings and that, even if she cannot speak to me individually, she speaks about us all as a world. I wrote before that I selected the poems in this anthology because they brought me pleasure. But if pleasure is and can be so variable, what does "pleasure" in poetry mean to me now? If I was charmed by the world each poet created for me that reflected, in some surprising way, my own at the time I first read them, what if the world I lived in now had changed so drastically the poems had become anachronistic?

No poem needs to anticipate the future to justify its emotional hold on readers. We apply the sentiments of a poem written in its moment in time to what we understand of our own; the poem exists in a continual present into which we step, not the other way around. During lockdown, I read the poems I chose again. I thought of all those poets out there, perhaps with their families, perhaps on their own, the unbearable solitude each of them was forced to experience watching everything change so quickly, perhaps irrevocably around them. At grocery stores, getting supplies, I experienced moments like this myself. A moment or two of piercing recognition—*this is not the life, the country that I knew*—and for a good few seconds I'd stand frozen in the aisle, tearful, almost panting. Then the dull veil of practical needs would descend again, and I'd walk on. I felt, in those moments, profoundly alone.

The poems I chose for this anthology did not comfort me. I did not want them to. And yet they still, strangely, offered me pleasure. If anything, these poems—and others that I read during lockdown—gave me a greater feeling and awareness of those painful shards of time. That lyric insistence of *now*, being present *now*; experiencing, through the reading of poetry, someone else's *now*. In another time that constant sense of the present might have felt oppressive, but during lockdown I came to find it liberating, because I couldn't imagine and didn't particularly want to think about the future, and recalling the past and all its mistakes made due to vacuous rhetoric filled me with a bitterness that verged on hatred. *Now* was fine; I could do *now*. I read the poems in this anthology like a string of rosary beads, each a little throb of prayerful insistence: This life happens. And this one and this one. A consciousness passes through the world and makes its mark. Now: I could find myself inside that adverb's endless, beautiful drift.

If we cannot treat this anthology as an objective experiment in excellence, or as an entirely accurate slice of history or culture, can we treat it for what it really is: a collection of *now*s, a way for us to connect our various experiences in time, to see where our own private forms of solitude and fear and love touch upon those of others?

Adrienne Rich's anthology was set against the backdrop of the American political crises of her day. And this anthology is, now, set against the backdrop of the global human crisis of our own. Rich's criteria for her anthology included a poem's willingness to address these crises explicitly, in ways that might defy the culture's larger contempt for language. For Rich, as for many writers, personal poetry was political poetry, and so she included work whose symbolism and syntax made them widely accessible. That is one form of American aesthetic politics, and it runs deep throughout the twentieth century. Another form, one that finds its roots both in late Romantic poetry and in modernism, and one that I find equally responsive to this contempt for language, is to insist on an imagery with the complexity and capaciousness to reflect the mutable sentiments of our moment. Though our aesthetics may be different, my project is not oppositional to Rich's; to me, they are two sides of the same coin.

Rich made her aesthetics obvious to the reader from the outset, something I think is important for an editor of this series to do. So let me tell you how these poems, even in my moments of crisis, were able still to delight me. For if I believe, as I wrote at the beginning of this essay, that pleasure is the only indisputable, if not objectively meaningful, measure of a poem's value, then the deepest pleasure I experience comes when I feel my sense of self expanded, my mind ideally changed. I take delight in poems as they open, continually, outward. I admire the writer's depth of metaphor that allows her poem to change as the reader changes, especially as the reader matures, which means that she can have a continuing relationship with a poem over time. The poems in this volume are ones I've returned to often over the course of this year, offering me a new way of responding to and reading them in each encounter. A poem that declares its sentiments for the moment limits my engagement by trying to insist upon the singularity of the poet's self and the incontestability of her meaning. It ages and dates itself by trying to curtail my interpretation. I outlast such a poem; I grow beyond it, because the poem requires that the conditions of my reading and the conditions of my belief be the same each time I read the poem for me to enjoy it. The poem becomes merely a declaration of sentiment, inspirational and not inspiring.

I take delight, too, in poems that have some fidelity to the real world and the ways the individual struggles to figuratively represent that world. They are poems that suggest the writer may not have a perfect understanding of how to capture her experience, whether it is the slipperiness of her mother's dialect or a father's decline into dementia, whether it is one's relationship to American wars abroad or to a particular constellation in the winter sky. These are poems that alternate between clarity and mystery in their use of metaphor. In the poems gathered here, I find objects and characters that are clearly depicted, while the relationship between these objects and the images they inspire requires me to search my own experience to see if the comparison is true. The poems move me because they rely upon my active completion of the metaphor: they require my engagement, not my passive acceptance of their ideas.

These poems also taught me that, even in their sense of *now*, they have a sense, too, of the past. These poems speak to and embroider upon the writers' own literary traditions. They have a sense of history—whether particular events that inform the poem or particular aesthetic conversations that made the poem possible. My pleasure in these poems, especially in those actively investigating their politics, stems from the writers' understanding that the present contains within it both a knowledge of the past and a speculation about, if not hope for, the future. The poem, then, seeks to create or at least acknowledge a genealogy of its crisis. A sonnet cycle examining the extrajudicial killings of black Americans, for example, gains part of its power by revealing how a wide array of poets, novelists, and public intellectuals throughout the twentieth century have written about this subject: what begins as a private lament turns quickly into a multivocal chorus of rage and loss. The poem, even as it speaks to its present, is never fully isolated in time, just as the poet is never the sole creator of the poem. It is not the poet's individual genius I recognize, but her affiliation with genius shared and shaped by generations of makers.

Finally, I'm moved by poems that have some investment in beauty, whether in sound or syntax, or in the fulfillment or expansion of their ideas. A poem about painting, a poem about sex, a poem about memory: all of these are, in this volume, the starting point for heady and often gorgeous speculation. Because I believe, too, that the intensity of thought an excellent poem inspires in us is a beautiful thing: beautiful because it is rare, and because it reminds us of the fellowship between people that occurs in language. When I read a poem, I read a mind and soul at work, I commune with them, as Walt Whitman might say, and I must activate my own language and body in response. When a poet grieves the death of a parent, I want to stand within, not apart from, that grief. And though I believe that as readers we should have a healthy suspicion of beauty in language, which manipulates us through particular effects, I also understand that we accept new ideas because their beauty attracts me to them. In that way, beauty does not have to be misleading or frivolous; it can be the vehicle for ideas and sentiments that change me for the better.

The poems in this anthology were chosen in one moment of time with these particular pleasures in mind. I believe these pleasures, and these poems, hold up; I believe some of the poems may even have a long life outside this anthology. And though I initially selected these poems for myself, I also knew they would be offered to you someday as a conduit: of expression, of amity, of citizenship, of love. That conduit has become more compelling to me now. Whether they are "best" or not, "American" or not, "poetry" or not to you, is less important to me than that they allow you and me, and you and these poets, to stand in some relation to each other. I offer these poems up, now, as an invitation. Inside each poem, you will find hundreds, thousands of others. Somewhere inside this expanding conversation, I hope your mind will be changed. I hope, too, you find some fellowship here.

THE
BEST
AMERICAN
POETRY
2020

Saving the Children

◇ ◇ ◇

Every day they were trapped, we checked in
with the nightly news to hear how
the Wild Boars were doing. A boot camp
had been set up at the mouth of the cave
after two divers discovered the boys
and their coach perched on a rocky ledge,
licking the walls for water, edging away
from the questioning sweep of the camera
as if afraid of exposure to the light
of the divers' flashlights, then bowing
in gratitude, their thin limbs,
reminiscent of children in newsreels
from the liberated camps.
                    We listened for updates:
volunteers pouring in—an Aussie doctor
stayed with them, checking their hearts,
their lungs, the ambient oxygen; a Danish
spelunker cut short his vacation to map
the underground labyrinth; a billionaire
built a mini submarine to float them out
of the narrow birth-canal-type tunnels;
ministers offered prayers, rescuers their lives
(one taken in earnest)—everyone working
together to get the Wild Boars out
before the rains fell and the waters rose.
                    But before we could switch
channels and savor the jubilation
of watching them saved from the worst
that could happen, trotted out of the cave,

wrapped in tin foil like baked potatoes
and rushed under golf umbrellas
to the thunderous sound of a downpour
of clapping into the waiting helicopters,
their mothers, aunties, grandmothers already
readying the meals the boys had requested—
fried rice with crispy pork, spicy chicken—
            we heard the crying
of children ushered into chain-link
enclosures, calling for their mothers,
their fathers, the wrenching look
of a toddler glancing up at the face
of a stranger speaking a language
she didn't understand—
            And we didn't understand
how this could happen: on the one hand,
saving the children, on the other hand,
wresting them from their parents,
as if we live in a zero sum world
where something has to be taken away
if something is put back together,
happiness being the give of a rope
that goes taut somewhere else—
where a body hangs limp
from the branch where the lynch mob
has strung it.
            It must be the fault
of such cruel mathematics, for how
else to understand this strange
disconnect, as if a part of us
we didn't know we had lost
in the fear-filled caverns of the heart—
the selves we discovered we could be
when we saved the Wild Boars—
were calling to us in the voices
of terrified toddlers,
in danger of being drowned out,
as the waters keep rising.

from *The Nation*

Customer Loyalty Program

◇ ◇ ◇

The opposite of not existing
is shopping. I am less the name
given me than my portion
of our nation's GDP. Student loan
interest rates and 401(k) projections
tangle on a graph, spurring one another
toward climax. I am my credit score
(777, which means I can afford
to gamble) by way of most common
denominator: the easiest consistent definition
for those who pass me on the street,
who sneeze into my collar, who walk
their dogs like their own sovereign nations.
The main export of dogs is love, because
that's all we'll take from them. I withhold.
I charitable contribution. I put into
a MEEK fund so I inherit whatever's left me
when the wars are done. Take
the whips and minimum gags allowed
by law and say thank you, chew
on the inside of my cheek. I am alive
when restrained, know my body
by what it pushes up against.
I am putting in my dues, stretching
my life out till next week's paycheck,
and the next; withhold a little bit
every other Thursday until
refund time, that time of year
all the S&M shops dream of, for we buy

new, plastic-smelling gags, we buy leather,
our own handcuffs. Will the nation
spoon us after? Do we need
SSN safewords? Are we expected to speak
with all this debt in our mouths, and what
would we say if it's removed?

from *Kenyon Review*

From "The Galleons"

◇ ◇ ◇

1.

Her story is a part of something larger, it is a part
of history. No, her story is an illumination

of history, a matchstick lit in the black seam of time.
Or, no, her story is separate

from the whole, as distinct as each person is distinct
from the stream of people that led

to the one and leads past the one. Or, her story
is surrounded by history, the ambient spaciousness

of which she is the momentary foreground.
Maybe history is a net through which

just about everything passes, and the pieces of her
story are particles caught in the interstices.

Or, her story is a contradiction, something ordinary
that has no part in history at all, if history is

about what is included, what is made important.
History is the galleon in the middle

of the Pacific Ocean, in the middle of the sixteenth
century, swaying like a drunk who will take

six months to finally reach his house.
She is on another ship, centuries later, on a journey

eastward that will take weeks across the same ocean.
The war is over, though her husband

is still in his officer's uniform, small but confident
among the tall white officers. Her hair

is marcelled like a movie star's waves,
though she has been too sick with the water's motion

to know that anyone sees her. Her daughter is two,
the blur of need at the center of each day's

incessant rocking. Here is a ship, an ocean.
Here is a figure, her story a few words in the blue void.

2.

Research is mourning, my friend says. Which means what,
exactly, for the things listed in the archives

as filling the galleons when they left Cebu and Manila—
ivory objects, jade objects, copper objects,

brass objects, lacquer objects, mother-of-pearl inlaid furniture,
pearls, rubies, sapphires, bolts of cotton cloth,

silks and gauzes, crepes and velvets, taffetas
and damasks and brocades, stockings, cloaks, robes,

kimonos, bed coverings, tapestries, linens, church
vestments, rugs, blue-and-white porcelain that numbered 1500

in one ship, wax, tallow candles, cordage,
sailcloth, musk, borax, camphor, cigars, varieties of tea,

cinnamon that was dried and powdered, 40,000 pounds of it
listed in one ship's manifest, cloves, pepper,

nutmeg, tamarind, ginger, Martaban jars from Burma,
Dragon jars from China, Vietnamese jars,

Siamese jars, Spanish jars, 800 jars found with the wreck
of one salvaged ship, jars that would have

contained tar for caulking, oil, wine, bizcocho bread,
salted meats, dried fruits, lard, bacon, beans, chickpeas, lentils,

flour, garlic, cheese, honey, rice, salt,
sugar, food for months, not enough food, not enough water,

chickens, cows, pigs, up to one thousand souls
depending on whether the ship had a tonnage of 300 or 500

or 1000 or 2000, ships that in the 250 years
of the trade route wrecked somewhere along the way

more often than they arrived in Acapulco, sailors,
mercenaries, officers, noblemen and their entourages, priests

and missionaries, slaves that were called *indios*
or *chinos*, nails, tools, iron hoops, fireworks, opals—elegy?

3.

We didn't want to be noticed, so we put charcoal on our faces.
I listen to the hours of tape, of the two of us at the dining table.

All the girls, looking like dirt. / My father was always drinking
Questions about the town, her parents, the names of people

or with women, my mother had to take care of the business. /
that only she could now remember. The images, I imagined,

My sister broke her back when she was a child, she grew up
scrolling in her mind, and translated into the answers she gave.

into a hunchback. She died very young. / They set up a dance
Sometimes pausing, not because she couldn't recall, but didn't

at the municipal tennis courts to celebrate the end of the war,
want to recall badly, the pause a kind of gap between what she

and he was there, in his US uniform. / He always insisted that
knew and what the words could do. The two things a voice

we sit at the front, but when I was by myself on the bus I sat
can say when it is saying one thing, the things that suddenly

somewhere in the middle. I didn't want trouble. / I was around
return when you are speaking, like pockets of color coming to

fifty-five when I had my first real job, working as the security
life in your mind: I listen to her with my skin and my eyes,

at Macy's. / I always liked to read. I wanted to go to college
my ears. I had had the notion that asking her about her life

like my sisters, but I got married. / You know that wedding
might add something to what I thought of as my art, as though

dress in the picture, we had to borrow it from our neighbor. /
her past and her love could be vectors of use. But I started to

I liked Japan when he was stationed there. It was so clean.
realize that what I actually needed to know, I would have

Then Norfolk. Richmond. / I was so sick on the ship, I can't
to conjure for myself, because what we know most deeply

remember much. Your mama just kept running all around.
we guard best, even as she spoke, laughed, passed the glow

It was a navy ship. / My mother's name is Canuta Sacay and
of each story to me, like a document I could have in hand

my father's name is Enrique Omega. My grandparents were
but could not understand. I put the tape away, felt for years

farmers outside Ormoc. / I was born in Ormoc, December 8,
that it was enough, the responsibility done. Our conversation

1924 or 25. / This was the apartment we lived in in Maryland.
stopped when my aunt came to take her out for some errands.

That's Junior there in the picture. And there's your mama.
Chatter, chairs moved around, then noises that are just noises.

4.

in Madrid I orient myself   I walk on the wide boulevards
and know an empire is its boulevards   I stand below the angel

skeptical of the beauty of angels   at the royal gardens I count
the 138 kinds of dahlias   at the crystal palace I imagine

the exhibition of plants indigenous to my islands   I walk
up the street of the poets   read the bronze lines on the ground

the longing and song of the pirate   in one museum I stare
at Picasso's lightbulb   in the oldest neighborhoods

I wonder if José Rizal walked these streets   studying diseases
of the eye during the day   writing his novel in the night

in another museum I look   at the paintings of the dwarves
of the horses   of the undying fruit   in the train station

I visit the memorial for the murdered   in the great white
square at dawn I walk   inscribe myself like letters on a page

at the naval museum I look into the face of Magellan   show the
painting my face   I sing the neighborhoods of Huertas

and Chueca   maybe only in Madrid   is the light a gold
weight always   at the supermarket I overhear   two Filipinos

speaking and I turn away and break   I find myself in
the cathedral   in the movie theater   where I watch a movie

without understanding the words spoken   around a corner
I stop because a kind of meadow   has been grown on the side

of a building   like a tallness of heart   a dream carried
into waking   my life breathing before it   incredible and true

from *Poetry*

Invention of I

◇ ◇ ◇

1.

In Farsi, I was given the name, but I wasn't a hero.
In English, I became a white man.

In Farsi, over 2,500 years ago, a new god was found.
In English, there is still only the one God. No one found another.

In Farsi, if you take bread from a verb, you make history.
In English, for a perfect past, it isn't enough to exist, you must have things.

In Farsi, the present isn't so simple.
In English, the simple past isn't so simple.

In Farsi, you can assume who's behind what happened.
In English, you need to catch them in the act.

In Farsi, enemy is the vice that ends with me.
In English, enemy is a friend that isn't me.

2.

In English, I was taught the author is dead. I was free.
In Persian, I learned fanaa: to kill the self and serve it to God.

In English, what you have doesn't follow you into the present.
In Persian, my past is imperfect.

In English, we capture with an army of nouns.
In Persian, we guard them with the veil of adjectives.

In English, "I celebrate myself."
In Persian, "Children of Adam are members of one body."

In English, we are proud and stand by what we do.
In Persian, everything gets in the way of our deeds.

In English, I hear the cuckoo asking "Who?" "Who are you?"
In Persian, I hear the owl asking "Where?" "Where is He?"

from *Copper Nickel*

A Man Drops a Coat on the Sidewalk and Almost Falls into the Arms of Another

◊ ◊ ◊

as in almost Madame Cezanne in Red,
almost falling, almost no longer—as in
almost only bent elbows, almost more
than longing, almost more than unholy,
more than skag, white lady, junk, almost

more than the city eclipsing around them.
Winchester Gun Factory's windows as broken
as the pair refuse to be, the two of them
nodding off of diesel, almost greater
than everything missing, the brown sugar,
the adrenaline slowing them down,
the remnants of a civilization emptied
into their veins. The falling man grasps
at the air. Lost in a trance.

These two, anchored by a coat that nearly
slips from a nameless man's fingers
as he leans parallel to the concrete,
as his arms reach for something absent.
Whatever about reaping. The men eclipse
the sidewalk, & everything else around
them & they sway with a funeral's pace.
These two, their bodies a still-life lover's

drag. I'm in the car with Nicky & we cannot
stop watching. I imagine one whispers *I wish
I never touched it*. But who, in the middle
of a high that lets you escape time utters
such bullshit. One lacks sleeves; the other
throws seven punches into the air
like an aging featherweight. I learned to box

because a desire not to be broken haunted
my dreams. And when Boxer throws six
jabs at a cushion of air, I know once
they both wanted to be something more
than whatever we watching imagine.

A car stops in the street. No hazards.
Just stops. & a photographing arm extends
the camera offering history as the only help
the two will get: a mechanical witness.
I photo them capturing this world slowed
to 15 rpms, the two men now a movie.
One almost caresses the face of the other.
Lovers are never this gentle, are never this

close to falling & never patient enough to know
that there is no getting up from some depths.
A perfect day that's just like doom. Own so
fucking world. They lean into each other
without touching. Horse has slowed down
everything. High like that, you can walk for

hours, & imagine, always that there is a needle
waiting for your veins. & Nicky says it's a wonder
how something that can have you hold another so
gently could be the ruin of all you might touch.

from *Tin House*

RYAN BLACK

Nothing Beats a Fair

◇　◇　◇

> As long as you're on the side of parks,
> you're on the side of the angels.
> —Robert Moses

Everything but the ice was carpeted—
the flight of stairs, benches and columns.
Carpet climbing the walls, stapled to plywood,

the sort bought by the roll, promising too many years,
too much of a discount. I'd look down from above
the scratched glass, the bad ice once home

to the General Assembly of the UN, where men
in neckties voted the partitioning of Palestine;
it was a skating rink before that, a skating rink again.

But the space still held the feel of what shouldn't last.
In 1964 a pavilion for Robert Moses's World's Fair
advertising "Peace Through Understanding,"

as though outpacing the Soviets in equanimity.
Walt Disney sold Mustangs and Pepsi-Cola
with animatronics and a twelve-minute boat ride

espousing interracial accord. Warhol showed the city
an image of itself: a twenty-by-twenty-foot silkscreen:
mug shots, our *13 Most Wanted Men*.

My mother served Löwenbräu at the beer garden.
Seventeen, she wore a French braid, a cotton dress,
and an apron at work. I imagine her train ride,

East New York to Flushing Meadows–Corona Park,
her transfer at Sutphin, then again at Roosevelt,
a bead of sweat starting at the hairline.

Or does she drive in with Roseanne,
someone with a real license and a used car?
I haven't promised a thing to the muses;

I can go on not knowing, so that on a Sunday
in August, my mother can leave for work an hour early,
after Mass. She can wear an A-line skirt, a gray plaid,

white blouse and stockings, black shoes pinched
at the toes. She comes to see Michelangelo's *Pietà*,
the jewel of Moses's fair, before her shift begins.

To keep the lines moving, and to keep the Madonna
and Christ at some remove, the pavilion erected
bulletproof glass and three motorized walkways

positioned at differing heights. She hasn't met
my father yet. She's seventeen. And what she'll remember
of the great sculpture—on loan from the Basilica of Saint Peter,

brought across the dark Atlantic, lashed with steel
to a liner's deck—what she'll recall is not
the blameless face of Mary, even younger than her own face,

or the pulses and veins of Christ's body so finely
wrought, but the lighting. The votive lights.
Cold. Directed. *Like an aquarium*, she tells me.

How fish seem so otherworldly in that blue light.
As it turned out, my mother never saw the *Pietà*,
and no one ever saw Warhol's silkscreen, no one

but the men who called for its removal.
Governor Rockefeller ordered the *13 Most Wanted Men*—
seven were Italian-American—be replaced immediately,

though the accused would remain, their *cauliflower ears*,
their scarred faces, specters behind a thin coat
of aluminum silver. *It's more me now,*

Warhol would say, staring up at the monochrome block
one year later. One year later the fair closed at a loss.
The New York Pavilion would go on unemployed

for the rest of the century, rusting alongside
the Grand Central, until given over to a memory
of winter, to Eddie Brown, the New York Stars

vs. the Green Machine. Eddie came from the Bronx.
He skated stiff-legged, upright. He was the only black kid
on the ice. *Blacker than the puck*, he'd say

to my brother on road trips. He was sixteen,
played left wing for the Stars, scored three goals
in two years. I was there for one.

I don't remember the goal,
a wrist shot or a redirect, a rebound chipped in at the crease.
I don't remember the period, the score, or much else

but the man who turned away from the ice
and to no one in particular said, *They let that nigger score.*
I was ten. I thought I knew who he meant;

the boys who carried box cutters on the J train,
who'd slash your face for nothing.
The ones my mother loved, in her school,

with razors under their tongues. The punch lines, setups—
So Al Sharpton, Jesse Jackson, and Farrakhan
are brought to Rome to meet the Pope.

The boys who stole Frankie's bike outside of Lane.
Fucked him up, too. My father just leaned into the railing,
his back hunched like a goalie's. He didn't flinch.

He kept his eye on the ice, on his son jumping the boards,
lining up for the face-off. My mother stepped back,
then seemed to harden like the women in those stories,

in *D'Aulaires' Book of Greek Myths*, who were
transformed because they would not give consent.
No one said a thing. No one answered. No one dared

question the man or the silence that wished
to make plain again the arena lights. An awful silence.
Tender. And easy to forget.

from *The Southern Review*

Bells

◇ ◇ ◇

Wind with barely a world in its path makes no sound.
And then the banner lifts and flutters. The one hand claps.

Bronze comes invisibly to life, and the startled temple
mourns the missing hand. Who here is not a child of bells.

They blow to song the abstracts of men through the open
garret. Who is it now, I wonder. And the bells turn back

to stone. Today I watched a movie of the killing. I thought,
perhaps, it would make me wise, responsive, or, in excited

horror, prone to see suspicion blown into a monster. I
am just one hand after all. A man is there. I do know this.

Bones of light, flesh of shadow, and as the gun goes off,
the wind of the known trajectory blows an abstract of men

through the open lesion. Who here is not a child.
Fire moves through broken windows and the figures in

a riot, and the names get taken down or lost. Night burns.
Embers graze the eye, but the movie does not change.

Characters are cast, in bronze this time, committed, bound
to mistakes they made or suffered or deepened by neglect.

Those who walk the tear gas go unseen. Some are pulled
aside, questioned, searched, and never found. Others

hang in the heart of the bayou like bells, and no one hears.
Some walk the pathless walk of bronze in the tower.

Forward and back, the stride of the breath and the broom
and the hasp of the flag beaten into wind and cinders.

However singular the bullet and path of light, the door
in the body swings both ways. In. And farther in.

The banner claps the air, and somewhere men prepare
the body for the viewing. Flowers release their ghost.

Overhead you hear the silence on which a music lies.
It is template-hard, cold, steady as the embalmer's table.

Say the widow is the one hand, her open bed the other.
The bronze that strikes her from her nightmare is the bell.

I have felt my own music overfill the vessel of the killer.
Whatever the misconception, it is looking for another:

a word to strike, a mirror, a wall. And now the movie
has come down offline. The children are sequestered.

The gun-metal river goes cold. Wind with barely a world
in its path fills and empties the needles of the valley.

Where there is a breath, there is an obstacle in its path.
America touches no one in particular and so a little of all.

It cracks as men in grief and office do. Every bell there
is two bells, one silent, the other made of words that so miss

the world, they ask, look. They break us open, and then,
in tired voices, break, so full of promise, they cannot find us.

from *Michigan Quarterly Review*

Orange

◇　◇　◇

My nail cuts through the peel, sends a burst
of oily mist through the sun splayed over
my aisle seat. The droplets move
in tandem, refracting the light,
and with the mist come bright citrus notes
that rapidly disperse into the olfactory systems
of surrounding passengers, interrupting their thoughts,
stirring awake the man in front of me
who hours ago told his seatmate *I'm taking*
a little valium. If you need to pee, climb over me.
He shivers, rubs his eyes. We speed into a knot
of clouds and before we're through he's asleep again.
Chipped ice sweating onto napkins mapped
with the country. An already-completed
crossword in the seatback. A game
I play with myself is to see how long
I can keep the peel as a single coil, its carpeted
underside, its surface pocked like a teenage face.
Each tear releases more droplets I admire
for how they seem to assemble and swell,
a plume that breaks apart with a kind
of intention, a mission, how I imagine chemicals
to operate in a medical context, dispatched into systems
of cells, trained to obliterate, defend, convert.
Depending on the light, some reach an almost
amber tone while others bleach to yellow
as if administered different dyes
like the slides of deformed cells
I studied three nights ago

while googling the specifics of my father's
leukemia, a browser window opened
onto paragraphs describing how
it's most common among California migrant workers
and those exposed to Agent Orange in Vietnam.
And yet my father stayed out of the war.
Another page showed photos of drum barrels
stacked in rows, each one painted with
a stripe of orange from which the Agent
gets its name. There's also an Agent
Pink, Purple, Green, Blue, White, called
Rainbow Herbicides. Because nothing
is too benign to be excluded from tactical use.
I see maps of dioxin production
include a plant in Newark, New Jersey
where a few miles inland my father as a boy
stood at his front door and watched
his father waking up hungover in the front seat
of his Ford where he passed out again
after a night at the VFW, a memory
inherited so long ago I can't remember
when he told me, or if he even did,
and yet it matures in shapes and textures,
the color of the car, the dewed grass shining,
high broken ceiling and easterly winds
blowing over from Newark.
I remember watching the war in black and white
in someone's living room, then in color,
my father said once. I searched for images
of scorched bone marrow and my wife
demanded I come to bed. I eat the orange
wedge by wedge, the pods exploding
between my teeth; wipe my fingers
on the seat cushion. I look up and see
on a seatback TV a few rows down
an aged Marlon Brando
as an even older Vito Corleone—
squirrel-cheeked, sitting among the tomatoes—
slide an orange peel over his teeth
and smile at his grandson who screams

and cries. He removes the peel,
laughs, the boy laughs, chases Vito through
the stakes, trying to spray him with a canister
of chemicals that mist over the family's
San Marzanos, then Vito coughs, staggers
through a pirouette, and collapses.
The boy thinks this, too, is a joke, stands
over the corpse, soaking its shirt with chemicals.
The cabin jerks. The seatbelt sign dings on.
A child behind me coughs. I hold my breath,
flash through panic fantasies of carrying my father's
death to him. In my head I hear the sentences
that describe how possible side effects
and genetic mutations can be passed down
to the exposed's offspring.
I read them once, then again, then couldn't stop,
wondering if I had just been introduced
to my death through reading, that it's already
in me, a blip on the end of an x-axis
just waiting for the data to catch up to it,
something I can google, read its Wikipedia page,
my death as a searchable item, inherited,
manufactured by the war, my death
the result of my country, already fraying
the edges of my cells, a future blankness
detected by scans, the war passed down,
the war inside of me. I stare down at the bare
wintered woods of the Alleghenies blurring past
and wonder if all the acres decimated
by the rainbow look like that, but all the time.
Rolling hills of brown trees give way to sprawl.
Pre-fabricated homes. Cul-de-sacs.
The oils moved like angelic flame,
the scent with incredible speed. I imagine
the phantom waves of messages I can't yet read
rising to my phone that say
we've been discharged and are heading home.
call us when you land. My father
shivering in the passenger seat.
Extreme nausea and aches, fatigue and low

spirits. I hand the peel to the flight attendant.
Gray flaps of wing metal rise and adjust,
a slight shift of the plane's axis.
My tray table is in the locked and upright
position. My seatbelt is low and tight
across my lap. I look down once more
at the mountainous dirt I call home,
then return to my book about the assassination.

from *The American Poetry Review*

Tender

◇　◇　◇

Then in the glass window of a streetcar, a godhead
Passes on, gone from this will for living on like a book

About a book, rote and morphinic
As a wet nurse travelling immune

With her small black bag on the train
To a minor city to feed some other's young

In the blush of antibodies, passing on.
Dear One, I have woken in the wingspan

Of a butcherbird, hung on the barbs of bad
Dreams like a metal rail fashioned out of thorns.

Odor of petrol, odor of hemlock bowing down, as the train
Passes from the city's circumferences of wire fence past

Recognition to an old World, I will be immuned
To knowing it. Do not forget this kind of tenderness.

from *Parnassus*

Obit

◊   ◊   ◊

Privacy—died on December 4, 2015.
My child brought a balloon that said *Get
Well Soon* to the gravesite. This time
Peter Manning lay next to my mother. A
stranger so close to her. Before this other
stone appeared, my mother's stone was
still my mother because of the absence
around her. The appearance of the new
stone and the likeness to her stone
implied my mother was a stone too, that
my mother was buried under the stone
too. On the day of the burial, I hired a
Chinese priest. I couldn't understand
many of his words because they were not
about food. The men who had dug up the
dirt stood with their shovels and waited.
I looked at their eyes for any sign of
drowning. Then I noticed that one man's
body didn't have a shadow. And when he
walked away, the grass didn't flatten.
His shovel was clean. I suddenly
recognized this man as love.

from *Mississippi Review*

The Waking Life

◇　◇　◇

It is rare for a person to enter
a castle, but common for him
to die there. Often enough

I feed the wrong meter.
One bird will raise another's
and think nothing. I raise

my head and am astonished
by the window's absolute
and complicated green,

the opposite of the wrong
suitcase's impassive empty
space. These are my hands

with nothing in them.
When all the trees and wires
have been transported

underground the birds will
have nothing to sit on.
Instinctively when sleeping

their talons clutch the perch,
as from an axe one would
attempt to save one's head.

from *Salamander*

Becoming a Forest

◇　◇　◇

Not to feel the grasses brush my knees, as if wading
for the first time into the ocean, but a different prayer—

this was after declaring, These trees are my bones,
and I could feel myself loosed from tendons, muscles,
and sinew, a skeleton knocking, as a chime
against nothing, and in my marrow
the blood of sap, the rungs of pinecones,
and myself, inside myself, telling me this—

to make an alphabet of stammering, a song
of a cry, to be anything buzzing with blood
or wings, anything alive, including grief, because
isn't that—I asked the trees, my bones' forest
framing me—what my long ago dead dreamed,
tossed in their short allowance of night?

from *The Adroit Journal*

MEG DAY

In Line to Vote on Our Future Climate

◊　◊　◊

Years from now—
　　　after the ice caps
　　　　　& the asteroid;
after the stars have died

　　　& we receive word
　　　of their passing,

but before the melting
　　　point has sung
　　　　　some lullaby
of mercury always tugging

　　　closer that sun
　　　we did not know

to fear; after the heat
　　　has become so rote
　　　　　we cannot re-create
much less recollect

　　　the feeling of cool
　　　or of breeze & even

stones quit carrying
　　　any memory of chill—

                    I will think of your
body cracked open

            at the center
            like the surface

of the Susquehanna
            in deep December,
                        the cool field
of your thigh against

            my cheek, the creek
            of me sprung cold

from sleep. I will keep
            for myself
                        the moment
before all this: the sand

            & the wasteland
            it made of us—

the day we woke & green
            in all its iterations
                        had abandoned us
& with it the earth—after

            the famine but before
            the drought, when

you fed my wet breath
            into the hot terrarium
                        of you still chilled
at the edges by less natural

            disasters. Like
            the neighbor boy

who told you where
            in the snow you should

———
30

　　　　　put your bare hand
& for how long you should

　　　　leave it. How it was
　　　　returned to you still

fixed to your arm
　　　　　but so cold it
　　　　　　　　nearly boiled,
so blue it was ablaze.

from the Poetry Society of America

All Through the War

◇   ◇   ◇

I couldn't remember any of it any more than I could feel
the corporate brotherhood at work among my breakfast flakes
or in those protein shakes I drank to keep my strength up.

I couldn't feel the toxicity the way I thought I should:
little silver pinpricks in my liver and then all over my body
steadily proceeding to a brownout in my limbic system,

the not knowing when I was, if or where we were at war with
and for what reason now. All the time I stopped eating
meat again. I stopped eating sugar. I bought four watches,

each watch stopped. I bought a pound of raw rough bulk
lapis lazuli from Afghanistan and I couldn't stop my tongue
from licking a certain piece of it like a dirty blue wedge

of Toblerone to know how it would feel. As for time, I didn't
always feel right with it, especially when alone especially
by the sea, where time widens to include more of itself,

partly because of the motion and partly because of sound,
which is also motion. A decade of drone strikes in the north
couldn't stop Pakistani street vendors from salt-roasting

sweet corn in pans like steep-sided woks. My eyesight grew
worrisome, I felt light tingling in my extremities and left cheek
I imagined meant diabetes, but it turned out to be nothing.

I turned out to be fine. Last week an airstrike in Somalia
targeting an insurrectionist youth group killed a dozen or so.
Yesterday they seized a village in the center of the country.

After my father's surgery, I went to Ireland on my own.
I told the lighthouse keeper I was worried something was
wrong with me because I couldn't stop looking at the water

with all its changing shapes and color. She said we are all
the same here love, all the same. Often in quiet I can still feel
the stone's abrasion on my tongue. I pulled a lichen from

the bronze age megalith with intent to burn it back home.
I made Syrian red pepper and walnut dip flavored with cumin
and pomegranate molasses. There is nothing more delicious

when eating this. How many seeds did Persephone take?
I thought I could cry for my friend no further until I opened
her armoire to lay to rest her scented shirts in an appliance box:

white, off white, shell pink, true pink, lilac, lavender, blue.
As polar seas warm up, the shrinking difference in air pressure
between the poles and the equator weakens the jet stream

and makes its path wobblier, explaining all this erratic weather
we've been up to. The senate voted against the resolution
to stop support of the Saudi intervention in Yemen as Trump

took lunch with the Saudi crown prince. I wake with scratches
I can't explain. I order herbal supplements at night online
and forget what for by the time they get here: ashwagandha,

schizandra. I read objects are more like events with longevity.
On average 130 Yemini children died each day last year
of extreme hunger and disease. A Saudi blockade on seaports

stops the ships delivering aid. These are casualties of war.
The instant the technician's needle found a vein, the seascape
on the wall rattled uncontrollably. She whispered the clinic

used to be a funeral home. Trump showed the prince posters
of the assorted planes, tanks, ships and munitions his oily
billions might buy him like an infomercial in the Oval Office.

What use is an adaptogen when I worry my own daughter
should soon prefer the hazards of an underworld to those of this
and social media? I dropped a fossilized trilobite in the toilet

and it cracked in half. Millions of years of structural integrity
finished just like that. Without Persephone it all froze over.
No crops grew. It was almost the end of us but Zeus her father

pulled strings to get her back. This service won't reactivate.
I have come to love catachresis because what's wrong with it is
right: I light my heart with so much emptiness there's room

here in the dark for everything. War-related violence in Libya
left 47 civilians dead this May: 38 men, three women, four boys,
and two little girls to dust returneth. One version of the myth

says Hecate leads Persephone to her mother with torches
at the end of winter. Mother with torches at the end of winter,
some days I just sit back and watch things tear each other

apart. It is winter on and off now through the end of spring.
Emotion is everything and nothing. Same is true for structure.
I said to my daughter on the phone: Be an honest person,

just be an honest person. Be honest, be honest, be honest.
Some days I can't believe what it means to be alive some days.
Some days I think about tearing myself apart but not exactly

with pleasure. Some days I know the strongest feeling is grief
but I believe it must be love: it has to be, has to be, has to.
Some days I feel each cell in my body has its fingers crossed.

from *New England Review*

HAZEM FAHMY

In Which the Devil Asks Me for My Name

◇ ◇ ◇

Marching on a dirt road to
Jerusalem, the Devil
bares his white
teeth, smiles widely

for me, asks if I would like
to live deliciously. I
say I live by the salt of

my sea, and that is enough.
Dissatisfied, he asks me
for my name. I say a name

is a proper pronoun, so
he asks if I am proper.
I was raised to be, but this

place I am heading is not,
rather rambunctious in its
joy. He asks me for its name,

a name is a title, is
a sequence, a lineage of
ash turned back to fire, call it

a heritage of boisterous
brick. He asks my mother's name
and I say it is a boat

        out of a burning country.
        He asks of my country's name
        and I say it is the song

I hear when everyone stops
singing. He asks me to name
a song, I say a name is

        dirt politics, failed econ,
        the way a military
        government is run, also

walked. A name is a date,
        is 1919,
        is 1952,
        is 2011,
        is 2013,

is other years I do not
remember, is other years
I don't want to remember.

        A name is a name is a
        nomad, without country, but
        a name is country, also

correspondent, is displaced
foreigner with a helmet
and a whole lot to say. A

        name is saying nothing you
        do not know already. The
        Devil bears his white teeth, asks

me about his name. I say
it is a name, which means it
is nothing to note, and yet

        everything to write. It is
        the Mercator map and the
        Manhattan Project, also

the mountain on which Yam drowned
gripping the flooding earth. I
bare my teeth for the Devil,

        and he smiles cold and long. The
        sun shines on his cracked skin as
        I keep walking.

from *The Asian America Literary Review*

The Shore

◇   ◇   ◇

In a nondescript hotel in East Texas, I fell
in love with a couple. There in the dim

hallway with rugs that were clean enough
but darkly patterned to hide the stains so who knows,

her back was against the wall, her arms up and around
his neck. He was bent down to kiss her, to press

his body into hers. Their bodies were fluid, two waves
not crashing but moving through each other—

I watched my friends from the other end of the hallway,
surprised, I had halted. Doesn't another's passion

make us want the same? They never saw me. I didn't stay long
and stayed silent. She was not his wife, but his

love was palpable. His hands were tender not quick.
Slow not furtive   That press.

I have been a witness to such passion more than once,
more than most. On a common street in Manhattan,

in a nondescript restaurant whose patrons—too young, too
childish to value discretion or quiet—spoke in loud voices

and fell drunkenly over the tables, I saw my dinner partner
through the oversized windows. The street lit by random lights.

He drew her up into his body. She was no friend of mine.
She followed me to follow him. She found him

and drew his face down to hers. They kissed in a way
that said they had kissed many times before and

perhaps it had been a long time. The kiss was long
and deep and I ate my steak au poivre bloody under sauce

and waited for them to finish, for him to come back
to the table after rushing out "to take a call."

They never saw me watching. Didn't even look up.
He swept her up as if his entire body longed

for a certain kind of completion. Her hair so like his mother's
he might have cried into it. Where is the shame

in that? She was not his wife. I am not his judge.
I was on the shore, only a witness to the oceanic:

dangerous, tidal, reckless, and always.

from *Virginia Quarterly Review*

Little Death

◇ ◇ ◇

after Jonathas de Andrade

When a man traps a fish
he removes the hook from its side
and once it has beaten its fright
into the wooden boat with its strongest slaps
he will clutch the fish to his chest
and hold it as it struggles
he will hold it in the tender air
He will hold its tail as if it were his dance partner's waist
and gaze into the fish's face for many minutes

When a man seizes a fish, he soothes it
caresses its whole body tip to tip
while it thrashes bloody against his bare chest
He will clasp the fish with one hand
like a newborn
and hush its gasping with the other
With love he will tuck it under his chin
so he can feel its heartbeat
in the insistent heat that hangs above the water

Remember: when a man captures a fish
he will seduce it while he slaughters it
the strength of his love can't be simulated
the sound of the green water can't be simulated
he will kiss the wheezing gills

his kisses can't be simulated
he will hold it as it struggles
that little death
he will hold it in the tender air

from *The Nation*

JULIAN GEWIRTZ

To X

(Written on This Device You Made)

◇ ◇ ◇

On the last day of September, a 24-year-old migrant worker . . . jumped out of a window of a dormitory run by his employer, Foxconn, the huge electronics manufacturing company with a million-strong workforce that makes the majority of the world's Apple iPhones.
—The Washington Post

1.

Pick it up.
Black glass our mirror when it's
off but it is never
off. Press home button
now. Flex. Press.
My fingerprint my hot oils is that
your finger pressing the button into place now on
assembly line in Shenzhen
before it's wiped clean
I see you I think I
see you load your
poem onto it, into me, into me now   *Did you, just like that, standing,*
fall asleep Did you fall farther than you meant Did you
mean me to be reading this *I want*
to touch the sky/ feel that blueness so light/
but I can't do

42

any of this/ so I'm
leaving this
world/ I was fine
when I came/ and fine when I
left   In this blue touchlight
fine rain starts
scrolling down

2.

On the contract, there are four options. Two show you will consent
and two show you will not. Do not tick the options which indicate you
are not willing. Tick the two which say you are. If you tick the boxes
which say you are not willing, the form will be cancelled.

3.

What do you see? Under
razorbright lights
blue hats blue jackets
every identification card
taken away long ago you
came 28 hours by bus

Rules are: no long nails
no yawning no sitting
on the floor no talking
or walking quickly no being
late no transients or preteens
no families   *If you doze off*

and fall against the machines and
there is a live wire no one will
save you The workshop
still as a ravine in autumn
when you slump and slide
back off your stool it's

a hare breaking out of the
underbrush

4.

Workers have up to ten minutes for visits to the toilet Such visits are
possible only if a supervisor is available and willing to stand in for
the workers on the shop floor The toilets are equipped with cameras
When a worker's time is up a loudspeaker calls for him by name until
he returns He returns For now

5.

That night rain's pouring into
                                    the underpass
fills up to the brim—cup of opaque
liquid crystal display—frame—shield—

If you get lost in the city you will be
replaced *I have people lined up to
replace you* $1.85 per hour no errors

Now you turn your head to see
                                    the train coming
rain torn by wind, unstoppable rain, fetid rain
It's scentless They rinse your uniform so many times
                                    it's scentless

6.

I pick it up. I ask it Who made you *I don't understand*
                                    Who was the person
who put this phone together *Do you mean call history* Was it wiped

at the factory or after How many hands touched it before mine *I don't
know myself but I can find out* I breathe in it's your air

44

7.

Motherboard left
your village you
miss her free
garden of plums
ravenala   *a language*
of tightening
screws Do you type
your poems into it

lychee   verbena   bougainvillea
eucalyptus   asbestosflower

at least three screens
a minute at least
twelve hours a day
spray the polish
onto the display
then wipe it dry
if you leave a trace
wipe it again

ten more nets go up

8.

The delegation comes to visit the factory the city government seeds
the clouds to cause rain it rains it clears the smog it leaves behind
blue skies from the ground silver iodide rockets fly up into the clouds
which condense which fall towards earth: raindrops. The air tastes
harder. The light sleeker. A frozen glass is rinsed in milk.

9.

Eighteen, your name meaning Walk Forward,

triple-bunked twelve to a room fences ten feet
tall on the roofs

                                bedsheets full of ash
dried gum in your fingerjoints and burrs
pricking behind your right shoulder

When you place it in its box
                              do you imagine me.

In the testing area the belt keeps running never stops
halfway through the sixteen-hour shift you recall
a corner of roof where one's torn   be quick—

Eighteen your name meaning Walk Forward
Eighteen meaning unfree meaning
                          falling from a great height

10.

You are the one
who installs front
camera with proximity
sensor leaning
over the factory
assembly a shadow—
sensor gains awareness
six hands later in process

but you figure out how
to turn it on early   *What if
there were a faint summons
they could feel*   Sensor makes
a square around your
face and focuses   *A pair
of hands gently opening
a red lacquered door*

11.

"On his rare days off Xu Lizhi likes to visit bookshops, lingering in the aisles. He frequents the factory library, and writes poems and reviews. He twice applies unsuccessfully for desk jobs—as a librarian at the factory and at his favorite Shenzhen bookstore Youyi. When a local journalist asks him about his future, he says: our lives will become better and better."

12.

I pick it up with my free hand, screenshot, Xu Lizhi, you're
standing on an overpass in Shenzhen, green plaid shirt,
your right hand holds your left forefinger,
                     you look older than
anyone your age—light traffic below and the railing's covered
in stickers, phone numbers . . .
                   I hold you in my hand you can't feel
proof of single status physical exam card   wastewater pours into the river, paystubs
scurrying like minnows   *certificate of conformity*   can't be both a boy and
a worker, choose one   *They've trained me to refuse to skip
work, refuse sick leave, refuse to be late, refuse to leave early—*

Shenzhen once a fishing village   children laugh dashing past
green lychee trees hulls heaped trash and scrub hills above
where now stands a bronze statue of Deng Xiaoping *a corridor
made of nonfiction*   When it happened no one   was there to see it

ten more nets go up

13.

You are the one
who changes air

filters in the manager's
office   the yellow-

stained black-caked
filter   a seine

that catches night in itself
all night

14.

I pick it up, type in your words   *A screw plunges to the ground*

working overtime at night   Another worker's falling asleep on the line

iron moon   head jerking   *It drops straight down with a faint sound that draws*

no one's attention   just like before on the same kind
                                        of night a person—

ten more
and grates on every window

15.

The boy breathing
next to you 120mm
tweezers turning thin

fingers the smallest
parts he moves by
hand always wears

gloves to touch it
until one morning he
picks it up and

types into it   *My eyes are*
so tired they won't open

16.

I look at it. Locked. Is there space for a distress signal if you wanted

to leave one. I switch silencer off, hit home, it gives me

only one emergency call, no private numbers, but it can take

a picture. Will record whatever I do next. *I've heard there's a time*

difference with foreign countries, here it's daytime, there it's night—

Designed by Apple in California Assembled in China Model A1549
FCC ID BCG-E2816A IC 579C-E2816A IMEI 355790070868852

17.

I pick it up

forgive me

I pick it up

from *Harvard Review*

Birches Are the Gods' Favorite Tree

◇　◇　◇

From one birch, a divine coppicing—the gods' trees
grow like teeth straight up, though some bend over
like Frost's boyhood branches—these ghosts
from an underground milky universe, a river under a river.
They erupt like teeth from a large-mouthed Being,
birches of the bottom lair become birches in the air,
as I once thought teeth were the ends of bones.
Is this gift enough, a white-rooted system for the pining few?
The torqued bush branch sails by with searing knots.
White and peach birch bark curls into clown wigs,
or the paper cuffs on the bone-ends of roasted lambs,
those belted girths of ribs, tied into meaty crowns.
A friend believes, after drawings, birch trees constitute
                              the largest Being in the world,
meaning a world under our world, one we cannot see
with the eye, made of telephonic roots connecting continents
like spider's silk or the long-reel shot-casts of molds.
Now, quiet by the creek, a collection of dirty ghosts.
Our little wood, at the bend, by the ugly houses,
near the field now a cul-de-sac, birthed out one sterile
birch unable to seed a grove inside the maple trees—
one lightning strike instead of an entrenched church.
We stripped its white bark off and touched the pink part
thinking "salts to the raw" and how much that would hurt.
We thought of the two rivers inside the birch's trunk:
Up, A Heaven River, beside a Downway, Hellward one.
One world beside another, waters different and together,

meaning a heavy river flows under the lighter one.
Which river spat out the white dog, skinned alive?
Shocked to be so stripped, especially around its eyes?
The dog, mottled fat-white and hemorrhagic red, walked out
from the slaughter pit to play, hesitant, humiliated, raw.
He walked towards us, wretched and confused, now naked
under the sun. On command, the good dog sits on its sticky
haunches, its white fur boots cuffed loosely at its paws.

From *Copper Nickel*

Sex

◇ ◇ ◇

It is hard to make this choice
when the room is so small and bright,
and the outside big and deep.
But I have not taught myself
to lie on the earth and feel
how much greater it is than me.
And I can't help following the sky
with my eyes as it moves past me,
and I can't help closing my eyes to imagine
the boat that carries me to the middle
of a lake as dark as the gaps between the clouds.
I forget everything I have learned
about how to hold myself
at the last edges of sensation
when not so long ago I held
the small hands of a child
and taught her to play a clapping game,
when I stood before a storm of scalding water
that would have killed me
if I gave it the mistake it looked for.
After all this time, we still must love and eat,
and none of us is alone.
See why I create these places where I am a stone.
In the bed, soft against the side
where I make the dark blanket more beautiful
and the sheet a pale and magnificent drawing,
there is nowhere to wrap the part of myself
that understands the handshake of joy
in my arms and hold her while she cries.

The sink is running in the next room
and the walls are flashed with what the world does at night.
Too much of us is evident in this hour
and I am sick with a cold fever
that hasn't broken since I was a girl
who loved how good it was to sleep
on the floor, so near to the silent ground.
Still, the boat, and the dark water
that has its private depth.
It never tries to carry me anywhere.
It makes the wind wait in the trees.

from *Poetry*

It Cannot Be

◇ ◇ ◇

undone. As here these words cannot be taken back into the windless wide
unsaid. No. These changes to the living skin of silence, there where your dis-
appearance into nonlife, into no-longer-ever-again-in-life—no—no longer in
creation, no, no more of your kind—changes silence to what can I call it—ex-

tinction—expiration—this new forever—the small boy on the boat in the dark says—says I
was holding you when we got on the boat in the deep night—says I can still feel
you now I feel you—others are pressed against me but this weight in the dark it is
you—I feel for your legs your feet—are you you or are these the pressings of

others—others are not me—once in a while a flashlight but so brief we cannot
be seen. Then it occurs. It cannot be. And *never again* arrives—is it for you or
me it arrives—the moment that cannot be undone. And we are no longer ever again in life
together. Mother. I need you. I cannot be taken back now into the unmade un-

conceived, unborn, back. You. As here these words live in the world you left behind. It is not
the world exactly, now. It is the now. That new world. *Now.* My body keeps living here
under my mind, slackened by thirst. I see light flick and I say to the air I still have
you. I have surfaces and wandering. Like a root always becoming more by going

on. The blackbird in the thicket understands me I think. It shoots through vacancy & knows
all is down to size, direction, speed. I could not find you, I wrestled the men who thought
to rescue me, me who am dead now, I said where is my mother to death which is a
wave, alive, contagious, & scent of brine, & seagulls slicing and feeding—such a soaring

machine. I spent with her a night my hand too tiny for her to find I think though I
touched and touched hoping day would take me into its teeth, interrupt this glassy
hammering of voice and sea, we are mangled, heaps, there are so many ways to be
afraid, it's all right, we were locked together in years, if we don't land again let's not

land again. But don't leave me. I am a work in the turning galaxy at the bottom of
this dinghy, I am a word that cannot be taken back, I want a home, how many inches is
a home, the gulls pull the day aside so I can see, I need a place to be, please not this
camp, this film of sand on me, the dry day's lip, everywhere tin's shadow-splash across my

only face. . . . Abundance where are you. An inch is enough. Moon and a vacant field
with no fear. Normal chimneys with morning-smoke. Water. Enough water. The shape of
water as it falls. Into my hands. To have a bucket of my own. To watch a long time the
water and feel there is always more. To not be afraid of sun. Of wind. My fingers remember,

I wish they would forget. I put them in the water that is not here. I can put them in that
water. It is a special kind. I have imagined it. Therefore it lies so still upon reality. It cannot
be undone, this water without a voice screaming to me of morning arriving
gradually and sharply, as if a fever lifting, dawn like a hand on my forehead saying the

fever broke, today will be a different day than yesterday, the cloth damp now over my
eyes, day is the simplest phrase, I can hear outside the unevenness of the stones, it is our
village again, light spliced by the cries of birds at dawn, I can hear the sand on the
road heading off towards the village, hear oranges pressing against their skins in their still-

living trees, hiss of morning coming on, I have not imagined it, it's day, we have not left yet,
it is not yet decided, drought touches the side of our house, shade is the simplest phrase,
a goat brays in the distance, which is not too far, then wind, it is the simplest phrase, it has not
said we have to flee, the froth of the goats' milk into the bucket is whispering the

simplest phrase, the broken surface of the well, where the wheel turns, the bucket rakes,
I hear it land, I should not have been afraid, I was not afraid, there was no
fear, ancient toughness lined it all, we were submerged in time not history, you take
your hand off my eyes and lift the cloth. The cool is good. It cannot be undone, it

cannot be unsaid unmade unthought unknown unrecognized untrued. Until it can.

from *The New York Review of Books*

On Patmos, Kneeling in the Panagia

◇   ◇   ◇

we hear the sound of a woman's high-heeled
     shoes striking the stones of the floor,
confident stride, strong hips, & I am
     back in a hospital bed at Clark Air

Force Base, the Philippines, September,
     1969, hearing a pair of shoes tapping their way
down the corridor outside my ward. I'd been
     knocked off a motorcycle by a drunk jitney

driver in Cavite City five days before,
     left leg shattered, compound fractures,
bone left on the street, flown to the surgeons
     at Clark who cleaned, debrided, sutured

& hung me up in traction. There were three
     of us in the ward. An air force guy
had blown the fingers off his left hand with a
     homemade bomb. He'd been at Cam Ranh Bay

at a party on the beach. Stupid, stupid, he said.
     The other guy was army, only seventeen,
right leg gone below the knee, left arm
     just above the elbow. Out on a routine

patrol his first week in-country, stood up to pee
     & the other newbie, pulling first guard,

shot him. They'd gone through boot together. He spent
       his days with a model ship, awkward

as it was to snap the pieces off & glue them into
       place one-handed. If I can do this, maybe
I can put myself together again, he said. Each night
       after lights out, he cried for an hour, softly,

into the snot on his pillow. The staff shrink was pissed
       I wouldn't say yes to amputation, said
I was immature. By that time I was hooked
       on Demerol, my butt cheeks already bared

at the stroke of each third hour, ready
       for the needle. End of that week,
late, they wheeled in three gurneys, jammed
       them tight against the walls, woke

us up. One held an army captain, left leg just
       a stump. He was hyper. Twitchy. Talked
a nurse into a telephone, called his wife. I'm fine,
       sweetheart, just fine. I'm coming home, voice cracked.

He didn't mention the leg. Second guy was nothing
       but plaster & gauze, both arms in casts, slits
at eyes & mouth. He didn't move, didn't make
       a noise. Third man didn't have any sheets

over him, only a gown. Both legs gone, left arm missing
       nearly to the shoulder, rubber tubes in both
nostrils, a pair of IV bags hung on posts
       from either side of the gurney. His mouth

was open, eyes glazed. He made a sound like a pair
       of house slippers shuffling across a bare
carpet. His catheter bag was half full.
       One of the volunteers came in the door

just as the orderlies left. They were officers' wives
       for the most part, helping out while their

husbands flew supply runs or medevacs, stabilized
        patients, wrote long, exacting reports. The war

was far away, except for the wards. They fetched us
        decks of cards, looked for paperbacks,
helped us fill out daily menus, poured out
        cups of water, let us flirt a bit, ignored our looks

of lust. This one looked tired. She talked with
        the captain, who still seemed buzzed, his hands
fluttering like bats. His stump thumped up
        & down as he talked. His top sheet was stained

brown. He kept repeating home, home, home. I heard her
        say the plane would load & leave real early, he
should try to sleep. She put a hand on his
        forehead. He settled, closed his eyes. She

moved on to the gauze man, but didn't do much
        more than stand. She reached a hand as though
to touch, but stopped, adjusted the edge of a sheet
        & turned away. She murmured something low

to the third soldier, put her ear down near
        his face & nodded. She took a cup of ice
from a stand, carefully placed a chip between
        his lips & let it melt. She did it twice

more. Anything I can get you, soldier? Her voice
        was soft. He made a groan, like
a rusted nut coming loose on a bolt. Yeah,
        he said, I want some cake, a chocolate cake.

She watched as water dribbled down his neck, said
        What? He said it again. She shook her head.
I'm sorry, she said, but you can't eat. She tried to give him
        one more piece of ice. Lady, he said,

Jesus, lady, I don't wanna eat it. I just wanna look
        at it. He clamped his teeth down hard

grinding away at pain, turned his head to
        the wall. A minute more, she left the ward,

gone for the night. Then it was another shot
        for me, lights out again & sleep. They came
before breakfast, the nurses, changing linen,
        bags, IVs, a single bed pan. The same

orderlies took the captain first. He waved
        at us when he left. Then they took the white
ghost who never moved or spoke. That was when
        we heard the click of high heels out

in the hall & the volunteer walked in, dressed
        for a date, strapless bright green gown,
blonde hair hanging over bare shoulders. She was
        carrying a cake in two hands, a big round

three-layer cake, a single candle lit. She walked to
        the soldier's gurney & stopped. He heard
her coming & turned to look: the froth of chocolate
        same color as his skin. They didn't say a word.

The orderlies returned. One checked the blood
        pressure in his remaining arm; one
changed the flow on both IVs. The soldier
        raised the stump of his arm, let it down

soft on the rumpled sheet. His nose & eyes
        were leaking. The orderlies released
the gurney's brake & wheeled him out. She took
        a few steps back to let them pass.

We saw her shoulders shake. She stayed like that
        a long, long time, then turned & left
without speaking. The candle had gone out,
        left a trail of smoke, like a fighter jet

leaves across a clear sky. The guy who blew off
        his own hand said, She could have left us

some. But it was all right. We couldn't have eaten
      the smallest bite of that darkness,

as here, on a Greek island thousands of miles
      & more than forty years away,
I wait for the bread of the body, kneeling
      beside a woman who feeds me every day.

from *Prairie Schooner*

Big Gay Ass Poem

◇   ◇   ◇

On a train coming home from work, my butt brushes the stomach of another
    man.
The train is crowded, & he is standing behind me.

In this moment, the contact feels alluring:
given the crowded train, the heat, the molding yellows of the train's interior.

A voice behind me calls out, "Hey man, c'mon. You don't need to rub your ass
    up on me."

Then, "What are you, gay?"

★   ★   ★

At first I wonder if what I've done commits me to the life of a sexual harasser.
Except it isn't me that rubbed the man's stomach; it is my butt.
My butt, the sexual harasser.

I think about the life that a sexually harassing butt might lead.
Rubbing itself on every surface that stimulates. A doorknob.
The flat, warm surface of a rock in the sun—
enjoying its warmth the way a sexual harasser might—
as indicative of another's hidden being,
forced into contact with my butt.

★   ★   ★

I think about the question the man asks me—*Are you gay*—and its answer—*yeah*.

I think about the unusual truth of it—
the predicament the insult creates—
how it lugs itself through its rhetoric;

the only answer appropriate to this question is—
no.

★ ★ ★

Is the comment more hurtful to me because:
A) In the casual way in which anyone speaks to another
on a rush-hour B train, he means to hurt
using the lowest bearing fruit one man can lob at an other.
I am the lowest bearing fruit.

Or is the comment less hurtful to me because:
B) To hurt me in this particular way, with these particular words
have followed me around,
like a kid brother
all my life: half its own person,
and half me through mimicry.

★ ★ ★

The man, disgusted by my ass, burrows his way into the crowd.

★ ★ ★

My ass is unmovable.
It is a gay ass.
A hot luscious piece of cherry-picked gay ass
best described by gay men with an emoji keyboard as 🍑

You are a peach, big gay ass, but
you are also a sexual harasser.

★ ★ ★

I think of all the places my big gay ass might have placed itself in that subway
    car, at that time.

Why there, in that man's stomach?
Had the big gay ass been attracted to the man?
Felt the need to rub its big gay assness into him?
The man isn't my type—having too large a beard, but

★　★　★

perhaps the big gay ass is lonely.
We both are.

★　★　★

The big gay ass had moved into the man's stomach to make room
for a woman, wearing a sunny yellow cardigan hanging loosely from her
    shoulders.

Although she wore it gallantly, cape-like, she herself seemed sad.
Sad woman, shrunken into the cardigan
like a sun turtle pumping its choad-like legs cautiously across a lawn,
ear holes peaked for a dog bark, the *swish swish* of a lawn mower.

Perhaps the big gay ass wanted to make room for the woman
with her pretty cardigan who seemed shrunken into the train wall,
amberized like a mosquito in midflight.

The big gay ass, which just that morning had seemed to fit nicely into its pair of
    ash slacks
but now seemed to push against them, using the big gay thighs as leverage for
    their escape.

★　★　★

Had the big gay ass not rubbed into the man at all?
But rather grown into the man,
spreading its big gay assness like a climbing ivy might?

Was the big gay ass getting bigger—gayer—all the time?

Like a gremlin from the movie *Gremlins*,
perhaps this big gay ass drew gayness in,
then doubled.

★ ★ ★

When the big gay ass & I waddle off the train, onto the platform,
and then slip through the door into the greasy New York night,
a group of small straight children seem to swirl around it

drawn towards it, but on their way elsewhere—
swirling with such coordination,
the big gay ass and I might be Marilyn Monroe atop a subway grate:
me, pressing down my hands to keep the big gay ass from sight,
the kids bunching and flaring around me.

Then their father walks by,
saying to his wife,
"creciendo."

★ ★ ★

Creciendo, big gay ass,
Thy Name is Creciendo.

Creciendo-ing like two loaves of warm brown bread
left to cool in the sun.

Creciendo and I pass the closed down gas station on our way home,
the gas prices now so old, they suggest some bizarro-America,
where the gas was cheap and the living was easy.

The gas station, empty this morning,
now harbors a grasping dirt pile—
a big gay ass dirt pile touching everything it sees,
growing into the terrain around it.

Big gay ass dirt pile,
Thy Name Too is Creciendo.

★　★　★

The big gay ass and I walk home—
past the bodega with its skull-colored lights
the sidewalk crack that resembles a toy train,
to our big gay ass home.

The big gay ass and I take off our ash-colored slacks,
and we write a big gay ass poem,

on a night as tender as a weed-whacker
grinding into the withered earth.

from *Fence*

Good Mother

◇ ◇ ◇

Praise the woman who took me in her arms &
wouldn't let go of me. We sank to the floor
in the middle of the aisle in Rite Aid.
It was a late morning & I walked slowly,
furious that spring could still be so wonderful.
Magnolia tempted me to forget about my mother
for a few minutes. I stared at a Brooklyn blue sky
through branches clasping pear blossoms.
The limbs shook in sunlight. My eyes adjusted
when I went into the pharmacy & realized
everywhere I looked the world announced
it would soon be Mother's Day. Something
ripped itself out of me. A howl so wide
I thought I would burst. The woman near the counter
understood right away the way my mother
once understood I had been born in a specific sadness.
The woman did not say she was a mother but I knew it.
She put her arms around me & waved away the cashiers,
the security guard who repeated Ma'am, Ma'am?
A stranger rocked me in her arms, so much kindness
as we fell over & crashed against a row of votive candles.
She didn't say it would be okay. She didn't ask me
what was wrong. But her arms put me in a vicious prayer.
I almost bit her, almost pushed her away.
We held on. We held on & praised the nameless thing
that makes us what we think we aren't strong enough
to know. She knew. She didn't let go of me.
Praise the woman who didn't wipe my snot from her shirt,
my tears from her collarbone, who did not tell me to

pull myself together while everything inside me dropped.
Crushed bones. Blossoms pushing through my mouth—
a word: *Mom Mom Mom*. This broken birdsong of mine
with no bird, no wing, no way to fly back through time.
Praise the woman who did not leave me
like something suddenly dead on the sidewalk
with a breeze blowing over its face.
Praise the woman who smelled like fabric softener
& coffee & the good things I must believe I am too.
Praise the mothers who walk slowly through the world,
bringing children into themselves, burying children sometimes
before themselves, & who defend something harder
than innocence. Praise the guts & grace of mothers.
Praise their exhaustion & their good work. Praise their wit,
their wonderful ways of listening to the world fall
asleep against its clean pillow. For the woman
who knelt with me in an ugly heap in the middle of
Rite Aid on an unbearable spring day,
who helped me buy a Mother's Day card
for my dead mother, who knew better than to say
I'd be just fine, for you I lift my arms each spring
& wish you a kindness so fantastic I sometimes feel
I'm in midair, the shadow of my wings clapping in joy
above your children who must love you.

from *Tin House*

The Conversion of Paul

◇　◇　◇

—for Paul Otremba

Bewildered—something in me is made wild
from looking at it—but something
also chastened, subdued, because
it holds my gaze a long time. It is itself
a unit of time—one bewildering instant
caught by Caravaggio's imagination—Saul
thrown off his horse, landing on his back,
taken aback, *Saul becoming Paul*, struck blind,
being spoken to by the light. It seems
none of us really cares for Gunn's
take on the painting, defiant insistence
of being *hardly enlightened*, but I admire
the chiaroscuro-like contrast he makes
between Paul's wide open arms
and the close-fisted prayers
of the old women he notices in the pews
when he turns away. But even if
Paul on the ground is *still falling*, both
are gestures of *blind faith*, as Stan calls
it. You call it *a bar brawl*, all this one-upmanship,
but in your poem you don't take sides,
you give your own perspective, twenty-first century,
postmodern, belated. You ask what happens if
a hundred people hold the painting in their minds
at the same time. *Will it gain a collective dullness,*
a tarry film like too much smoke? But I like to think
it would sharpen the focus, deepen the saturation

of the red cloak, crumpled like bed sheets, beneath him.
A lot could be made of how Gunn, then Stan, then you
make a poem out of a painting, but Caravaggio
did it first, making the painting out of verses
from the Bible. All art traffics in some kind of translation.
Which might be another word for conversion. God says
Saul, Saul, why persecutest thou me? It is hard for thee
to kick against the pricks. Which makes me think
of the horse, who should be more visibly
shaken probably from such a flash of light.
No one seems to register how claustrophobic
it all is, difficult to believe it's happening
outside, where there should be space
for all this stretching out, and the horse
wouldn't have to raise one hoof so as not
to step on Paul. And the groomsman,
why isn't he doing anything but
staring down? Like all Caravaggios,
it's sexual, the arms and legs splayed as if
ready to be taken by God himself,
but it's really an outsize gesture of shock.
I heard the news of your being sick, Paul,
when I was in Italy. If God himself
is the radiance that struck Saul into Paul,
then what is the darkness swimming around
everything? It makes one feel inside of something,
confined by such dark. Afterwards, the Bible says,
Paul *was three days without sight, and*
neither did eat nor drink. Now after chemo
you consume a thousand calorie shake
called The Hulk to keep from losing weight.
I went to see the painting when I was in Rome
in September. It is a pleasure to look at a painting
over time. To consider it along with others,
including you, my friend, over decades.
Something in the painting is insistently
itself, intractable, and yet inexhaustible meaning
keeps also being revealed. Paul, thinking of you
when I look at the painting changes it. I see you
vulnerable, surrendered, beautiful and young,

registering that something in you has changed
and what happens next happens to you alone.
And inside you. Conversion is a form of being saved,
like chemo is a form of cure, but it looks to me
like punishment, a singling out, ominous,
and experienced in the dark. When
I used to see the painting, I was an anonymous
bystander. Now I am helpless. It is
and you are, in the original sense, awful.
I can't get inside the painting
like I suddenly and desperately want to,
to hold him, to help you get back up.
And now, for Paul, everything has changed.

from *New England Review*

During the Middle Ages

◇ ◇ ◇

O God I am so fat
I cry all the time
A kitten scrubbed with a toothbrush online makes me sob
I'm so heartless seven species of bees
Are now endangered and I didn't do a thing
Didn't even send any money
To anybody doing any good
And I can't lose any weight I skipped yoga
I'm so hot all the time so broke
So pathetic no wise investments
Should've bought a 7-Eleven on a busy corner
When I was seven or eleven
Nobody wants to lick my neck
Nobody wants to hold my hand at the doctor's office
Nobody to grow old with me I'm so crabby
To pluck my beard feed the cat I don't have
And read me endless Russian novels at night
All the ones I still haven't got to so greatly depressing
Where are you handsome? Are you
Driving in your car to come visit me
Bringing a bottle of wine & a present so gallant?
A new translation of Akhmatova? I love it!
          No? Well, I guess it's better than living
In the real Middle Ages when
Some shithead priest threatens you with hell
To pocket your last coin and there's no Tylenol
So you have to suck on some skullcap seeds
And knights canter about knocking you down
To take your maidenhood with pointy lances

And you have to work as a midwife with no birthing tub
Nobody washes their hands or votes
Nobody knows about DNA or PMS or NASA
There's nothing to read even if you can read
Except boring doctrines or *Spiritual Exercises*
By Gertrude the Great, I'm not kidding
Yes, there's Dante Chaucer and some sagas
But it's not like you'd get near those books
You'd be lucky to have some jerk recite
The latest by Wulfstan the Cantor by campfire
Right before he beheads your uncles
And forces you to rub salve on his abs
You know you'd be sweating in a wheat field at twenty-two
Dying from your tenth pregnancy by the bailiff
Courtly love?
      Not a lot of it I bet
Some local doctor would have to drill a hole in my head
To let the demons out because I'd be full
Of Black bile plus heresy as I am today
It would be an awfully hard time
When the sun revolves around the earth
And kings are unbelievably selfish
The Roman Empire fell flat
Vikings disemboweled your cousins
And the Lord of the Manor thinks you're cute
And it'll be a very long time before Pop Art
And meerkat videos and cotton candy
And sexting and fish tacos and girl bands
Everything's just so bad and you have buboes
      Hopefully I'd get shoved into a nunnery
To have an ecstatic experience with mystical Jesus
Or better yet, I could be a hardcore samurai
Laying down justice on the heads of corrupt lords
But that was tough work, dirty work
You're working for nobility who at any period
In history are the worst people in the world
And to be an unemployed ronin had to bite
Sunday afternoons no mom around to make you soup
Even if all the brothel ladies want to scrub your back
Sometimes you only want a nice nap

And some Neosporin on your wounds, ah
            If only I could be like the divine Sei Shōnagon
Resplendent in silks with seven-layered sleeves
Writing in my room about politics, gossip, my lovers
Listing Splendid Awkward Adorable Annoying things
Things that Make One's Heart Beat Faster!
I wish, okay, I could be her devoted servant
Tidying her papers and fluffing her pillow
But even she found many hateful things
About living in the Middle Ages
Like crying babies messy guests and mansplainers
So irritating even way back then
You better shut up and take your medicine

            from *The Iowa Review*

Putting the Pieces Together

◇   ◇   ◇

Not what it usedtobe, doesn't mean
it can't be something now, and so
Anna glued the pieces one by one.
Didn't someone say that beauty
was the orphaned daughter of perfection?
Glue or grief—both harden—but glue
you can find in a store. Your fingers adhere
to my hip. My lips press against your neck.
By some measure, we are brave.
By older measures: Baby, ya'll
ain't gotta licka shame. But the choices
we had are the choices anyone has:
alone, without, or take the serpent's apple.
Adhere any two parts: what you saw
and what actually happened, a midnight-blue
soup tureen in the Azores and the one
in the china cabinet in my dining room.
Apply pressure. Add adhesive or add here
a black woman, a white man, a road map,
and a potato peeler. Hue adheres to human.
And the things we adhere to make us over
into their own image. They often make you
repeat loudly, "She's my wife." I worry
that they'll bury us apart. Here an eye
used like a cop's baton. There the woman
who kicked us out of her house. You haven't
heard a word I said. This is about the soup tureen.
I was explaining that skin can be boiled for glue.
Use a potato peeler, or a paring knife. Remove

your skin, boil, and bring to simmer. Apply
skin glue to anything broken, or what
might be broken, to anything you want to save.
Muay Thai fighters break their shins against banana
trees, kicking the trunks over and over. Their bones
grow as hard as concrete. The two of us—like that,
the microscopic tears, repeated healing and repair.
Even a broken soup tureen will carry a story.

from *Poetry Northwest*

Sunday at the Mall

◇ ◇ ◇

Sweetheart, if I suddenly flop over in the mall one afternoon
while taking my old-person-style exercise
and my teeth are chattering like castanets,
and my skull is going *nok nonk nok* on the terra cotta tiles
                        of the well-swept mall floor;

my tongue stuck out, my eyes rolled up in my head—
Don't worry, baby, we knew this kind of excitement
might possibly occur,
and that's not me in there anyway—

I'm already flying backwards, high and fast
into the big arcades and spaces of my green life
where I made and gave away and traded sentences with people I loved
that made us all laugh and rise up in
unpredictable torrents of fuchsia.

Dial 911, or crouch down by the body if you want—
but sweetheart, the main point I'm making here is:
don't worry don't worry don't worry:

Those wild birds will never be returning
to any roost in this world.
They're loose, and gone, and free as oxygen.

Don't despair there, under the frosted glass skylight,
in front of the Ethiopian restaurant
with the going-out-of-business sign.

Because sweetheart, this life
is a born escape artist,
a migrating fever,
a convict tattooed in invisible ink,
without mercy or nostalgia.

It came down to eat a lot of red licorice
and to adore you imperfectly,
and to stare at the big silent moon
as hard as it could,

then to swoop out just before closing time
right under the arm of the security guard
who pulls down the big metal grate
and snaps shut the lock in its hasp

as if it, or he, could ever imagine
anything that could prevent anything.

                    from *New Ohio Review*

Fifteen

◇   ◇   ◇

The Fall of the Rebel Angels
Pieter Bruegel the Elder, 1562

[*Terrapin!*] [*Tentacle!*] In the atrium
    Brightness my sons'
  Delight presses so close

To the canvas the guard coughs a caution.
    The commotion
  Of wing and fang that is Bruegel's *Fall*

Of the Rebel Angels hangs like a trespass,
    [*Claw!*] [*Carapace!*]
  Like a curious cabinet

Had sex with a scavenger hunt. [*Salamander!*]
    Halfway headlong
  Down his hurtle one handles

In his demonic fist a fishbasket
    Finned with switches.
  Another faller fledges

Into swallowtail, the fleshy edges
    Of his lewdness
  Startled with butterfly finery.

A third [*Hurdy-gurdy!*] is girt with the garnet
    And sudden gold
  Wings of the lucifer bird,—

Every peculiar pursued to its foundering
                Is part something
        Else, [*Armadillo!*] [*Esquire!*]

As agog at itself as at an ambush
                        Of angels. My angels,
                Half-plunged into each your own strangeness,

Gangly and almost in need of a shave,
                [*Amphibian!*]
        [*Astrolabe!*] as the transiting sun

Through the windowpane frames you momently still
                In your mutual
                Conclave of puzzle and name

I observing can guess why the heavens
                Mustered, taking
        To trumpet and frantic buckler:

Some with swords would arrest that reverseless
                [*Pufferfish!*] fall,
        Holding fast their once familiars

By force. But see, in the ether—a flourish
                Of brasses, a mass
        Of seraphs suspended, weaponless.

I suppose those horns clarion not in discord
                But in blessing,
        A benediction on the dim,

Bewildered way ahead, which as yet
                They do not know,
        And so cannot regret.

        from *The Cincinnati Review*

The Garden
of Earthly Delights

◇   ◇   ◇

Because order matters: breakfast, then lunch,
then dinner, dessert following the main course;
the orgasm, yes, but the foreplay before;
old age, yes, but first youth:
Dante's *Divine Comedy* only considered
a "comedy" in so far as it ends
in Paradise, having first given us
a grand tour of the Inferno and then
Purgatory, as methodical if not
quite so easy as A, B, C;
so that, when we look at Bosch's *Garden
of Earthly Delights*, it matters whether
we read it, as readers of English will tend to,
from left to right, beginning in Paradise,
where Dante's masterpiece ends,
then passing through that ebullient garden
bursting with the planet's abundance of pleasures
on the way to that culminating, grotesque,
and, one assumes, irrevocable final
destination, the grim fate that we, in Dante,
climb out of—we, that is, the readers,
the viewers, the detached, impartial observers,
carrying the passports that permit us safe passage
into and out of these unearthly zones,
and not, by any means, the internees,
those who have been granted, against their will

and without their asking (though Dante's Virgil
would have disagreed, insisting that they did,
in effect, ask for this, that they did indeed will it)
permanent residence status—or whether,
in fact, we read it in some other way,
as, for example, presenting these
three states of being as being suspended
before us all at once, as if,
at any moment, we might slip partially
or even completely into any one of them,
or, for that matter, as if at any moment,
an elemental intrusion from hell or paradise
might erupt, without warning, into our lives—
so that the story is not a tale of causation
(sin leads to hell, light to darkness, delight
to damnation) but rather a manner of grasping
the complexity of our existence, how things
that are opposite, if they do not attract,
at the very least coexist, taking place
in one and the same moment, the disparate
constituents of human life that do not,
as one might have expected, when brought into contact,
annihilate one another, but instead,
by the very force of their contrast, heighten
and strengthen each other. What, other than evil,
could make virtue shine so bright? What, other than
purity and naïve hope, could entice
corruption and despair into bursting forth
to appear so nakedly as what they are?

Because order matters, yes; but our lives
are not orderly. And art, precisely
because it is, feels at times like a mere
detached imitation, yet can also feel
as if it were more like life than life
itself. Which is why, one assumes, we are drawn,
again and again, to the place where the picture
hangs, to stand in its presence, as if
it were only in those moments that we lived.

But we come from elsewhere, and we go elsewhere
when we are done with our looking. That they
are *earthly* delights, indeed, reminds us
that Dante's *Commedia*, too, begins
not in hell but on earth: that famous dark wood,
not a garden of delights, not at all, but a kind
of garden nevertheless, and that
an arrival in Paradise might well take
the form, as in that remarkable final
shot of Tarkovsky's *Solaris*, of
a return to Earth, a real Earth or
a reconstructed Earth, an imagined
garden or a painted garden, or simply
the garden where you were born. The leafy
globe, perhaps, that we see when the triptych
is closed. It is the earth that is ours,
and Dante's cosmic love, though it moves
the stars that track their paths through their skies,
is a leafy thing, a fleshly thing,
a thing of the soil, a thing that demands
to be lived out on this surface, on the face
of this terrestrial sphere, this local
unheavenly orb, this, our planet,
our neighborhood, if, that is
to say, it is to be lived at all.

from *ZYZZYVA*

ILYA KAMINSKY

In a Time of Peace

◇   ◇   ◇

Inhabitant of earth for forty something years
I once found myself in a peaceful country. I watch neighbors open

their phones to watch
a cop demanding a man's driver's license. When a man reaches for his wallet,
        the cop
shoots. Into the car window. Shoots.

It is a peaceful country.

We pocket our phones and go.
To the dentist,
to buy shampoo,
pick up the children from school,
get basil.

Ours is a country in which a boy shot by police lies on the pavement
for hours.

We see in his open mouth
the nakedness
of the whole nation.

We watch. Watch
others watch.

The body of a boy lies on the pavement exactly like the body of a boy.

It is a peaceful country.

And it clips our citizens' bodies
effortlessly, the way the President's wife trims her toenails.

All of us
still have to do the hard work of dentist appointments,
of remembering to make
a summer salad: basil, tomatoes, it is a joy, tomatoes, add a little salt.

This is a time of peace.

I do not hear gunshots,
but watch birds splash over the backyards of the suburbs. How bright is the sky
as the avenue spins on its axis.
How bright is the sky (forgive me) how bright.

from *The New Yorker*

Sho

◊   ◊   ◊

a "torchon" after Indigo Weller

Some need some Body
or more to ape sweat
on some site. Bloody

purl or dirty spit
hocked up for to show
who gets eaten. Rig

Body up. Bough bow
to breeze a lazed jig
and sway to grig's good

fiddling. Pine-deep
dusk, a spot where stood
Body. Thus they clap

when I mount *banc'*, jig
up the lectern. Bow
to say, "it's all good,"

we, gathered, withstood
the bends of dives deep
er, darker. They clap

as I get down. Sweat
highlights my body,
how meats dyed bloody

look fresher for show
ing, I got deep, spit
out my mouth, a rig

id red rind. Bloody
melon. Ha! No sweat!
Joking! Nobody

knows the trouble. Rig
full o' Deus. "Sho
gwine fix dis mess." Spit

in tragedy's good
eye! "This one's called. . . ." Jig
ger gogglers then bow

housefully. They clap.
". . . be misundeeeerstoooood!"
Hang notes high or deep,

make my tongue a bow—
what's the gift?! My good
song vox? The gift?!?! Jig

gle nickels from deep
down my craw. They clap.
I'se so jolly! Stood

on that bank. Body
picked over, blood E
rato! Braxton's *sweat*

y brow syndrome®, spit
out a sax bell ~~wring~~
a negrocious show

of feels. Fa show, sweat
equals work. Bloody
inkpot of Body,

I stay nib dipped, show
never run dry! Rig
orously, I spit

out stressed feet. Lines jig!
Ha ha ha ha!!!! Good
one [that/I] is, bow

deep but not out. Stood,
shining, dim. They clap,
waves slapping hulls. *Deep*

don't mean *sunken*; *good*'s
not *yummy*, right?! Bow,
blanched with foam, jig-jigs.

"This one's called. . . ."—they clap—
" '_ _ _   _ _ _ _ _ _   _ _ _ _ _barrow.' So much dep
ends / upon / dead _ _ _ _ _ _ _" Stood,

I on that bloody
rise of sweet Body;
there *you* is, too. Sweat

it, let's. They clap—"Rig
ht?" some ask, post. Spit
tle-lipped: I said: "Sho."

from *Poetry*

I Never Figured
How to Get Free

◇　◇　◇

The war was all over my hands.
I held the war and I watched them
die in high-definition. I could watch

anyone die, but I looked away. Still,
I wore the war on my back. I put it
on every morning. I walked the dogs

and they too wore the war. The sky
overhead was clear or it was cloudy
or it rained or it snowed, and I was rarely

afraid of what would fall from it. I worried
about what to do with my car, or how
much I could send my great-aunt this month

and the next. I ate my hamburger, I ate
my pizza, I ate a salad or lentil soup,
and this too was the war.

At times I was able to forget that I
was on the wrong side of the war,
my money and my typing and sleeping

sound at night. I never learned how
to get free. I never learned how
not to have anyone's blood

on my own soft hands.

from Poem-a-Day

After,

◇   ◇   ◇

the orchards flowered. The fields
breathed out, like a lung. What
    expectation. After,

at the Peace Fence, veterans
    from North & South swapped belt plates
for the country's press corps. *Country,*

    they whispered, slipping it
across their tongues again as one
    might a finer shiraz. Some regiments

played banjo for their enemies. The president
    was alive still. Sherman
hacked the rice coast into acreage. As in

forty, with a mule. Imagine. After,
    black sheriffs. After, Easter
as emptied shackles. After,

    at supper, the McDonoughs
of central Pennsylvania looked up
    & watched their sheepdog—gone

two months, a minié ball
    bedded in her foreleg—resplendent
as fable on the porch steps. The moral—*America,*

good puppy. Good
deathless little dream-fiefdom. If
    for a minute— If

in ceremony merely— In Manhattan,
    after, in lapped serge, Southerners
marched lock-step, correct

    as a stitched line, behind the caskets
of Union generals. In Virginia,
    Lincoln read Shakespeare. Paused,

we know, at the moment—imagine
    the witches prancing, the woods
risen with their broadswords—sedition

    lay chastened & gasping. & after,
the cotton flourished. Freedmen
    practiced their signatures. After, fragments

of munitions shimmered in their cases
    like saints' bones. So bullets,
for a time, turned vintage. If

    in passing, if after
the worst one country could visit
    on a people was visited, history

dragged its scales to the Southland.
    Longstreet—Lee's
hand at Gettysburg, conductor,

    after, of black militias
in New Orleans—led them,
    armed, against a White League

one would recognize. For which,
    afterward, no statues
were erected. After,

from the ashes— After,
in America, *no masters*
   but ourselves the spangled banners

of schoolkids declared. In Carolina,
   after—the exact fairgrounds
the South had flaunted its stallions

   through, or had, of a Sunday, come to
in its veils & worsted—freedmen, wreaths
   of lilies in their arms, interred

the Union dead in excelsis. Sweetly,
   the mulberries ripened. Worms gathered. After,
we began—

from *The Georgia Review*

Bear

◊   ◊   ◊

Once it was clear he was gone,
everyone wanted to know
what was done to him,
his carcass, his emptied skin,
did it smell, they would ask,
and how warm
was the warmth of his last breath,
how long did the inside
of the skin stay warm, did it adhere
to touch, they would ask,
was he held against your body,
anyone's body, they wanted
to know about the meat,
what was done with it,
was it cut away, could they buy it,
was it available to see,
did it fester, turn green, did it smell
and like what, what did it smell like,
was it left for the dogs, cooked up,
cubed, or left skinless, muscle,
did he hide under the bed, they wanted
to know, did he struggle as he went,
did his loves, and when he loved, was it open-
armed, was it as warm
as his death, can we sing of his loves,
they asked, can we count his lovers,
and between shows, turning pale,
under thickness, his body, did anyone
know what his tired body was like,

they asked, was he crumpled in a pile
by the pike he was shackled to
when he was found, did he resemble
a large coat tossed on the ground
after a night of drinking,
or was he like a folded dress shirt,
ready to wear, did he resemble
loved ones they knew, was he
human, when everyone left him,
was he a human, was he dignified,
a small voice asked, did he die
a dignified death, do any of us?

from *The Gettysburg Review*

The Gift

◇ ◇ ◇

You can tell whether a bird has a mate
if there are pinfeathers on its head, new feathers
that start out as stubs full of blood then enshroud
themselves in a white scaly coat as they grow.
Preening releases the feather, but a bird can't reach
the top of its own head. A mate preens that spot
unless the bird is alone in a cage. Pinfeathers itch,
so I preen my unpaired birds: wrap them in a towel,
scritch their heads and blow till dandruffy stuff
flutters out. They looked pretty mangy this morning,
I recall, as I stare at the side of my mother's face
from the backseat. How long has it been since I
took her in for a haircut? And her whiskers—she can't
see to shave. We're driving back roads, pointing out
deer and hawks as she *ahs* before taking her back
to her apartment. Collin calls it "travelling gravel."
She loves it when he drives and I sit in the back
so she can talk as much as she wants. He always
answers her questions. Sometimes I'll go hours
without saying a word while she talks and talks.
When I was little, she'd bring a book to restaurants
and read while I, no doubt, talked and talked. Things
children said weren't interesting to her, she told me,
and family never had to say, "I'm sorry." Yes,
we've hurt each other, but only I've done it
on purpose. Did I tell you she bought me this car?
It's the most generous gift I've ever received.

From *Ploughshares*

The Jungle

◊　◊　◊

An Afro-Cuban plea guards over heart
　& head, that old rugged cross-tree
　　of the South in the tropical air of Cuba,

but it would take years in Madrid,
　then Matisse, & a daily dreaming
　　of Paris before Wifredo Lam

painted himself in a floral kimono,
　echoes of war tangled in his brushes,
　　before he could bring himself to half-see

those watchful polymorphic figures
　in gauche on Kraft paper glued
　　to cloth canvas smooth as second skin.

He said, "When I am not asleep, I dream."
　The land grew whole by brushstrokes,
　　an uproar of growth pruned back

to vantage point, the first time I faced
　The Jungle, big as a double door
　　to a secret realm. I close my eyes

to step into vegetable silence, living
　designs triangulated, into a kingdom
　　of spirit totems in bamboo, sugarcane,

tobacco leaves, & double-headed limbo
    growing one with the other, caught
        in a love fever of three worlds, a path

to the other side, hidden from the sun,
    relying on conjured light in a blue-green
        season, pelting the ground with seeds.

Did the "W" in his name etch the first
    winged symbol as indigenous signs
        & masks rooted in black soil?

Breasts, buttocks, & terrestrial mouths
    laugh in the greenery—we onlookers
        see magic we cannot face in ourselves,

reasoned beyond our own mortality
    enriching the wet-green profusion
        wild within itself & what cries out,

seeped in ceremonial lamentation.
    Tall figures hold sharpened shears
        as if shaping footsteps out of foliage,

gazing into a future, these maroons
    masked by zodiacs in their leafy hideout,
        a rhythm of breathing architecture.

A slew of bluish incantations erupt
    in carved silence, unwoven trance,
        & these elongated, slantwise warriors

& seers, the other side, hidden from us
    in daylight, interwoven & multiplied,
        peer out of camouflaged revelation.

He drew questions out of shapes,
    rooting shadows to the roaming mind,
        & this makes me take another step.

Exiled, but not from his homeland,
   orishas tiptoed back into CoBrA's
      inner sanctum. Vodun & Santeria

followed him to Marseille, still
   orangery-red touches of Caribbean
      sunlight on the skin of his figures.

Though once in a cabaret on *La Rue Vavin*
   he heard "I put a spell on you,"
      & a smile broke across his face.

from *The New York Review of Books*

NICK LANTZ

After a Transcript
of the Final Voicemails
of 9/11 Victims

◇   ◇   ◇

Au clair de la lune, mon ami Pierrot, prête-m—
the earliest extant recording of a human voice,
its warble brushed into lampblack with pig bristle
(the tune a love song masquerading as a lullaby),
fourteen years before Alexander Graham Bell
turned a cadaver's ear into a recording device.
Someone told me once that *hearsay* came from
heresy, because gossip was a form of blasphemy,
but I only have his word to go on. The ear hears
the past: the workman hammering, his hammer
falling a heartbeat before the sound reaches
a boy watching the construction from behind
a fence. I close my eyes, and I'm a child
sitting on the floor, listening to the fan
in my mother's darkroom or the noise of my father
at his lathe in the basement. That's all Bell's
dead ear recorded: a whoosh, a blare, nothing
recognizable. My friend composes music played
on empty bowls. A bowl can only do what it does
because absence is part of its structure. Maybe
that's obvious. It holds broth, or assorted fruit,
or decorative glass beads, or, yes, a tone.
You've heard that ugly trope about the native
who thinks the camera will steal his soul,

that there's something unnatural about
taking a photograph (we say *taking* after all),
but it's sound that isn't meant to be held.
Flowers wilt, their stems cloud the vase
with slime, so we replace them with silk
and plastic, the water with blue glass beads.
Most footage of atomic bomb detonations
is dubbed with generic explosion noises.
The truth is loud and ugly and disappointing
and arrives thirty seconds after the bomb
goes off, the Joshua tree in the foreground
swaying slightly. Some of the canned laughter
played over the sitcoms you watched
as a kid was recorded decades earlier, and surely
some of those original audience members
were long dead but still laughing at bad
jokes—the root of *joke* originally meaning
to speak, to utter, or perhaps to confess,
though you didn't hear that from me.
Every sound is the completion of a promise—
the broken window, the unhappy child—
an acknowledgment that, yes, the pain
was real. Someone far off heard it and glanced up
from what they were doing and looked
all around to see where the sound came from.

from *Copper Nickel*

On Faith

◇ ◇ ◇

There is no map for how the apples fall.
The tree feels nothing letting go.
Along the crumbling wall that holds the sun-
Baked orchard, shadows ease their way.

There is no map for how the apples
Fall. Silence in the house. The tree sees
Nothing looking out, lets go. I'm more
At ease among shadows than the wall

Of sun stalled above the house. I hold
The orchard, its walls, this silence.
Seasonal, it comes and goes, easing itself
Back into shadows. There's sweetness

In the crumbling, letting go, the how and why,
This sunbaked nothingness I feel
That comes, goes. What's sweet is sweet
In so many varieties, becomes nothing

After all. A wall is just a wall in wind
Or rain. A tree a tree. Silence in the house.
The apples fall. There is no map for how.

from *The Gettysburg Review*

STEVEN LEYVA

When I Feel
a Whoop Comin' On

◇   ◇   ◇

—for the feast of Whitsuntide & Afterschool Dances

ain't the butter
            fly, it's the tootsee
roll the speakers
            pose as a polemic
against your narrow hips

            this circle's musk
classmates grinding like
            black pepper in a cheap mill—
uneven, coarse. Shamelessly
            you practice outside

the arc of polo shirts, crop-
            tops and starchy jeans sharp
enough to cut penumbras
            from 8th graders. Summon
an adolescent faith to push

            past the girl who laid her tongue
in your mouth like a lisp on a field
            trip to the zoo right
in front of the rhino

exhibit. Your lonely Afro-
Latino blood bids

      the center of hype,
ooooooh, and funk to be
      filled with your inheritance—
flat feet, a skinny boy's sense
      of rhythm, and a soft uptown fade.

Go boy, Go
      you've only heard
in church. This dance is
      different than the holy
ghost shout filling half

      an hour on Sunday
nothing like the body
      rock of your father's bachata
he'd pull out to prove men
      with flat asses could dance.

Still you press and press
      throw your knees like bolos
catch up to the dj's scratch in
      time for the song to switch
choruses—Boyz II Men: *don't wait*

      til the water runs dry. Those
violins still weep for the awkward
      slow drags you'll soon try
but there's a two second panoply
      where you've imitated the other

boys in their non-buttered fly
      in their roll tout-suite. There
at least a hip moment of locomotion
      where no one could charge
you with a lack of blackness.

To the left, to the right
more flame than Pentecost,
          eyes like two upper rooms
wholly ghosted, your body
becoming a tongue, spoken.

from *jubilat*

Locomotion

◇ ◇ ◇

When tendency
    derails intent
(C4, C5 out
    of line) buckled
first thing by
    routine
sheet-smoothing;
    it's so
light, the throw
    that settles,
so divides
    a tensile spine
from one in throes—
    a while,
the tendons
    must have hitched
their ropes a little
    tighter behind
my back,
    their twang
I must have
    freighted
for days:
    each night
that froze &
    every
dawn over rotten
    train ties running
on but off—

a slip will shift
the time-
        table, stop
by junction
        locked, till non-
functional, un-
        coupled, out-of-
sync: what you
        do & say &
think. I did
        double down
every day; said it
        pained me
none; I thought
        nothing of regular
chafing at this
        body & no where
it carried me
        counted; now,
I count chipped
        discs of paint.
Lying in
        the bed I've made,
adjusting my old
        conditions
for bliss, clicking
        through this chain
of spine & side-
        lined, I'm fine-tuned,
I'm fine

from *The Sewanee Review*

Qassida to the Statue of Sappho in Mytilini

◇ ◇ ◇

Kyria, why do you stand askance, facing neither
    sea nor mountain,
not even toward your wild flower fields?

And the lyre on your shoulder was it meant
    to be the size
of the plastic jugs shouldered by Moria's refugees?

I saw them in Sicily too, home of your exile,
    where no rescue
could pause time's grating at their memories.

Your island is empty of poets, Kyria. I came
    to meet them,
to recall the trembling earth under my feet.

Hangers-on reporting to newsletters throng
    the cafes, researchers
hacking at fieldwork, polishing CVs.

The migrants are all court poets now. At night
    they labor to translate
their traumas into EU legalese.

Or sit at your feet shouting into cell phones
    to scattered relatives,
trying to crack the code of the model asylee.

Kyria, there's no way for me to see you, no date,
        or sculptor's name,
only fascist graffiti below your knees.

Why do your eyes glare lifeless like apricot pits,
        your stone body dim,
a paper lamp trembling in the breeze?

Or is that you now Kyria, holding Cleis's hand
        wearing hijab,
glad to be home again, not quite at ease?

from *Kenyon Review*

The Punishment
of One Is the Love Song
# of Another

◇　◇　◇

At last, I have found my assassin. At last,
I have struck gold. When my past hissed
with cobras, you let me sleep. When
I was falling, you brought the ground closer
and made gravity of flowers like a kiss.

One body moving is a seduction. One body
is a practiced leap and a parachute
unsprung. Only the scalpel knows the passion
of blood. We soothe it with cold and sing it
to sleep. We leap at the chance to be blistered.

We listen and stiffen. We pivot and reap.
My rib cage could be a wasp nest built
of paper. My hand could be the slip of sand
across itself to slake the great unknown.
Snow coughs along the windows now
and listens differently to the pure. Snow
brocades like cotton. Prayers, like burdens, go.

from *Waxwing*

Night of the Living

◊ ◊ ◊

If the constellation of stars
above your house looks like
a woman skating across a lake

you could name it that. If someone
long before you called it warrior with a sword
or dragon at the gate, it doesn't matter,

it's your sky now. If you're lost in the evening
fog all your former selves line up by the side
of the road to show you the way home.

If you want to pry open the moon
and crawl inside, remember the sky
waits like a clock for you to unwind.

The planets contain the fur of wooly
mammoths and fossilized ferns
that never got to be trees. Your position

relative to them is what you think about
when night is a rabbit hole and sleep
is a coin toss. A hand moves across your face

in a dream you are having about being alive.
When you wake up the hand disappears
along with the way it felt to be dreaming,

on the edge of some great adventure.
The shadows of owls against the trees
are not owls but you can pretend

the sound of branches against the window
is someone trying to get in. You can breathe
and imagine the night breathes with you.

from *The Commuter*

JOHN MURILLO

A Refusal to Mourn
the Deaths, by Gunfire,
of Three Men in Brooklyn

◊ ◊ ◊

And at times, didn't the whole country try to break his skin?
—Tim Seibles

You strike your one good match to watch its bloom
and jook, a swan song just before a night
wind comes to snuff it. That's the kind of day
it's been. Your Black & Mild, now, useless as
a prayer pressed between your lips. God damn
the wind. And everything it brings. You hit
the corner store to cop a light, and spy
the trouble rising in the cashier's eyes.
TV reports some whack job shot two cops
then popped himself, here, in the borough, just
one mile away. You've heard this one before.
In which there's blood. In which a black man snaps.
In which things burn. You buy your matches. Christ
is watching from the wall art, swathed in fire.

This country is mine as much as an orphan's house is his.
                                        —Terrance Hayes

To breathe it in, this boulevard perfume
of beauty shops and roti shacks, to take
in all its funk, calypso, reggaeton,
and soul, to watch school kids and elders go
about their days, their living, is, if not
to fall in love, at least to wonder why
some want us dead. Again this week, they killed
another child who looked like me. A child
we'll march about, who'll grace our placards, say,
then be forgotten like a trampled pamphlet. What
I want, I'm not supposed to. Payback. Woe
and plenty trouble for the gunman's clan.
I'm not suppose to. But I want a brick,
a window. One good match, to watch it bloom.

America, I forgive you . . . I forgive you eating black children,
I know your hunger.

           —Bob Kaufman

You dream of stockpiles—bottles filled with gas
and wicks stripped from a dead cop's slacks—a row
of paddy wagons parked, a pitcher's arm.
You dream of roses, time-lapse blossoms from
the breasts of sheriffs, singing Calico
and casings' rain. You dream of scattered stars,
dream panthers at the precinct, dream a black-
out, planned and put to use. You dream your crew
a getaway van, engine running. Or,
no thought to run at all. You dream a flare
sent up too late against the sky, the coup
come hard and fast. You dream of pistol smoke
and bacon, folded flags—and why feel shame?
Is it the dream? Or that it's only dream?

& still when I sing this awful tale, there is more than
a dead black man at the center.
                                        —Reginald Dwayne Betts

You change the channel, and it's him again.
Or not him. Him, but younger. Him, but old.
Or him with skullcap. Kufi. Hoodied down.
It's him at fifteen. Him at forty. Bald,
or dreadlocked. Fat, or chiseled. Six foot three,
or three foot six. Coal black or Ralph Bunche bright.
Again, it's him. Again, he reached. Today,
behind his back, his waist, beneath the seat,
his socks, to pull an Uzi, morning star,
or Molotov. They said don't move, they said
get down, they said to walk back toward their car.
He, so to speak, got down . . . Three to the head,
six to the heart. A mother kneels and prays—
Not peace, but pipe bombs, hands to light the fuse.

Fuck the whole muthafucking thing.
                              —Etheridge Knight

A black man, dancing for the nightly news,
grins wide and white, all thirty-two aglow
and glad to be invited. Makes a show
of laying out, of laundry airing. Throws
the burden back on boys, their baggy wear
and boisterous voices. Tells good folk at home
how streets run bloody, riffraff take to crime
like mice to mayhem, and how lawmen, more
than ever, need us all to back them. Fuck
this chump, the channel, and the check they cut
to get him. Fuck the nodding blonde, the fat
man hosting. Fuck the story. Fuck the quick
acquittals. Fuck the crowds and camera van.
You change the channel. Fuck, it's him again.

I enter this story by the same door each time.
                                —Julian Randall

At Normandy and Florence, brick in hand,
one afternoon in '92, with half
the city razed and turned against itself,
a young boy beat a man to meat, and signed,
thereby, the Ledger of the Damned. Big Book
of Bad Decisions. Black Boy's Almanac
of Shit You Can't Take Back. We watched, in shock.
The fury, sure. But more so that it took
this long to set it. All these matchstick years . . .
He beat him with a brick, then danced a jig
around his almost-carcass. Cameras caught
him live and ran that loop for weeks, all night,
all day, to prove us all, I think, one thug,
one black beast prancing on the nightly news.

Not Huey on his high-back wicker throne,
beret cocked cooler than an Oaktown pimp.
Or young Guevara marching into camp,
all swagger, mane, and slung M-1. But one
less suited, you could say, for picture books
and posters, slouching on a northbound Bolt,
caressing steel and posting plans to shoot.
He means, for once, to be of use. Small axe
to massive branches, tree where hangs the noose.
He says he's "putting wings on pigs today,"
wants two for each of us they've blown away.
Wants gun salutes and caskets. Dirges, tears,
and wreaths. Wants widows on the witness stand,
or near the riot's flashpoint, brick in hand.

I itch for my turn.
—Indigo Moor

Like Malcolm at the window, rifle raised
and ready for whatever—classic black
and white we pinned above our dorm room desks—
we knew a storm brewed, spinning weathervanes
and hustling flocks from sky to sky. We dozed,
most nights, nose deep in paperback
prognoses. *Wretched* and *Black Skin, White Masks,*
our books of revelation. Clarions
to would-be warriors, if only we
might rise up from our armchairs, lecture halls,
or blunt smoke cyphers. Talking all that gun
and glory, not a Nat among us. Free
to wax heroic. Deep. As bullet holes
through Panther posters, Huey's shattered throne.

Poems are bullshit unless they are teeth . . .
—Amiri Baraka

It ain't enough to rabble rouse. To run
off at the mouth. To speechify and sing.
Just ain't enough to preach it, Poet, kin
to kin, pulpit to choir, as if song
were anything like Panther work. It ain't.
This morning when the poets took the park
to poet at each other, rage and rant,
the goon squad watched and smiled, watched us shake
our fists and fret. No doubt amused. As when
a mastiff meets a yapping lapdog, or
the way a king might watch a circus clown
produce a pistol from a passing car.
Our wrath the flag that reads *kaboom*! Our art,
a Malcolm poster rolled up, raised to swat.

every once in a while
i see the winged spirits of niggas past raise out the rubble
                                                    —Paul Beatty

Could be he meant to set the world right.
One bullet at a time. One well-placed slug,
one dancing shell case at a time. One hot
projectile pushing through, one body bag
zipped shut and shipped to cold store, at a time.
Could be he meant to make us proud, to fill
Nat Turner's shoes. Could be he meant to aim
at each acquittal, scot free cop, each trigger pull
or chokehold left unchecked, and blast daylight
straight through. Could be he meant, for once, to do.
We chat. We chant. We theorize and write.
We clasp our hands, spark frankincense, and pray.
Our gods, though, have no ears. And yet, his gun
sang loud. Enough to make them all lean in.

Paradise is a world where everything is sanctuary & nothing is a gun.
                                                    —Danez Smith

A pipebomb hurled through a wig shop's glass—
nine melting mannequins, nine crowns of flame.
Hair singe miasma, black smoke braided. Scream
of squad cars blocks away. Burnt out Caprice
and overturned Toyota. Strip mall stripped.
And gutted. Gift shop, pet shop, liquor store,
old stationery wholesale. Home décor,
cheap dinnerware. An old man sprinting, draped
in handbags, loaded down with wedding gowns.
Three Bloods and two Crips tying, end-to-end,
one red, one blue, bandana. Freebase fiend
with grocery bags, new kicks, and name brand jeans.
Spilled jug of milk against the curb, black cat
bent low to lap it. This, your world, burnt bright.

I love the world, but my heart's been cheated.
—Cornelius Eady

He thought a prayer and a pistol grip
enough to get it done. Enough to get
him free. Get free or, dying, try. To stop
the bleeding. *Blood on leaves, blood at the root.*
I didn't root, exactly, when I heard
word spread. Word that he crept up, panther like,
and let loose lead. A lot. Before he fled
the spot, then somewhere underground, let kick
his cannon one last time. "One Time," our name
for cops back at the crib. It had to do,
I think, with chance. Or lack of. Chickens come
to roost? Perhaps. I didn't root. Per se.
But almost cracked a smile that day. The news
like wind chimes on the breeze. Or shattered glass.

We beg your pardon, America. We beg your pardon, once again.
                                                    —Gil Scott-Heron

To preach forgiveness in a burning church.
To nevermind the noose. To nurse one cheek
then turn the next. To run and fetch the switch.
To switch up, weary of it all. Then cock
the hammer back and let it fall . . . But they
were men, you say, with children. And so close
to Christmas. But their wives, you say. Today
so close to Christmas . . . Memory as noose,
and history as burning church, who'd come
across the two cops parked and not think, *Go
time? One time for Tamir time?* Not think *Fire
this time?* To say as much is savage. Blame
the times, and what they've made of us. We know
now, which, and where—the pistol or the prayer.

. . . like sparklers tracing an old alphabet in the night sky
—Amaud Jamaul Johnson

It's natural, no, to put your faith in fire?
The way it makes new all it touches. How
a city, let's say, might become, by way
of time and riot, pure. In '92,
we thought to gather ashes where before
loomed all that meant to kill us. Rubble now
and lovely. Worked into, as if from clay,
some sort of monument. To what? No clue.
Scorched earth, and then . . . ? Suppose a man sets out,
with gun and half a plan, to be of use.
To hunt police. Insane, we'd say. Not long
for life. In this, we'd miss the point. A lit
match put to gas-soaked rag, the bottle flung,
may die, but dying, leaves a burning house.

—Robert Hayden

But that was when you still believed in fire,
the gospel of the purge, the burning house.
You used to think a rifle and a prayer,
a pipebomb hurled through a shopkeep's glass,
enough, at last, to set the world right.
Enough, at least, to galvanize some kin.
Think Malcolm at the window, set to shoot,
or Huey on his high-back wicker throne.
Think Normandy and Florence, brick in hand,
a Black man dancing for the camera crews.
You change the channel, there he is again,
and begging: Find some bottles, fill with gas.
Begs breathe in deep the Molotov's perfume.
Says strike your one good match, then watch it bloom.

from *The American Poetry Review*

Chasm

◇

Monthly, my family calls from Vietnam
to inform us about the dead.

Their voices amplified through the speakerphone
while my mother sits upright in her bed

& performs a variety of mundane tasks:
sewing, word finds, removing nail polish.

Of course I want to assume things:
dead body, dead butter-yellow lawn—

If I try hard enough, I can gather
each story, like marbles, into my mouth

spit them into the drain & watch
                as hair climbs out.

Every month, a new body washes up
in conversation:

a great aunt, a dog, a cousin or two, but now
it's my father's first wife.

Four-days-dead in her bathroom
my uncle says

—she lived alone, abandoned
years earlier, by her husband.

Buried in a backyard
somewhere in that roadside village

the woman he left in Vietnam
to come to America

he promised he'd return
for her & their two sons

but instead married my mother.

—well, she was found dead.

Four-days-dead, in a bathroom
my father once built for her.

Buried in my uncle's backyard.
Had to kill the dog too.

It kept trying to dig her out.

Either anyone can be forgotten
or only the forgotten can bring

forth a good haunting, spanning
the chasm of the living, above which

a bridge made of ghosts, full of ghosts
waiting to be summoned through

      the receiver

one by one by one by dead one.
I can see them all
          gathering

in the pixelated air. A patch of light
ruptured by dust. I know my mother

will make a great ghost one day.
They love her, the ghosts. They watch her

all the time. She knows this, but she just sits there
unbothered, biting the seam of a white dress
until it splits.

from *The Massachusetts Review* and *Poetry Daily*

Hyacinth Aria

◇ ◇ ◇

When my mother was felled, by the sudden blow
of a stroke, decked by a deep bleed when the old
brain tumor broke through, and I flew
to her, and sang to her for the rest
of her life, for two days, sang her
out, they told my students where I had
been, and there on the seminar table
was a garden, in a small shoebox
crate, with a lattice wooden fence, in-
side it the spears of hyacinths.
This morning I leaned over her cut-glass bowl so
cut it looks about to draw blood,
and there in the water jellied with peeling
bulb-skin, down inside the thighs of the shoots, there was a
cunning jumble of bumps, rinds,
green mother grinds of hyacinths
soon to bulge, and rise, and open,
and, for a moment, I almost mourned
my mother—mourned her when she was a child,
a frail being like an insect, with papery
wings, with little, veined skirts,
before she had pummeled anyone,
before she had taken the cudgel from her own
mother to wield it in turn on me who would
take it in turn as my purple stylus,
my gold pen. And so, for a moment,

I loved my mother—she was my first chance,
my last chance, to love the human.

from *AGNI*

Letter to the Person Who, During the Q&A Session After the Reading, Asked for Career Advice

◇   ◇   ◇

The confusion you feel is not your fault.
When we were younger, guidance counselors steered us
toward respectable occupations: doctor, lawyer,
pharmacist, dentist. Not once did they say exorcist,
snake milker or racecar helmet tester.
Always: investment banker, IT specialist, marketing associate.
Never: rodeo clown.
Never: air guitar soloist, chainsaw
juggler or miniature golf windmill maker.
In this country, in the year I was born,
some 3.1 million other people were also born, each
with their own destiny, the lines of their palms
predicting an incandescent future. Were all of them
supposed to be "strategy consultants" and "commodity analysts"?
Waterslide companies pay people to slide down
waterslides to evaluate their product.
Somehow, that's an actual job. So is naming nail polish colors.
Were these ever presented as options?
You need to follow your passion
as long as your passion is not poetry and is definitely a hedge fund.
If I could do it over, I'd suggest an entry level position
standing by a riverbank,

or a middle management opportunity
winding like fog through the sugar maples of New England.
There's a catastrophic shortage
of bagpipe players, tombstone sculptors and tightrope walkers.
When they tell you about the road ahead,
they forget the quadrillion other roads.
You'll know which one belongs to you because
it fills you with astonishment or ends with you being reborn
as an alpine ibex—a gravity-defying goat, able to leap
seven feet in the air, find footholds where none exist,
and (without imagining it could ever be anything else)
scale a vertical sheet of solid rock
to find some branches, twigs, or wild berries to devour.

from *Waxwing*

Climate Is Something Different

◊ ◊ ◊

This was a heron, and the oddly effortless but dense wedge
its body made across the sky, and more odd for being unfamiliar,
landing on the puddled roof of the nearby frame shop,

the second day of the flood receding. Then, there was the crew
of red-vented bulbuls (which took me days of search terms
to identify—"black-crested bird with red breast," "bird with red chest,"

"bird red stomach," "bird" & "red" & "Houston"—when they invaded
last summer's ripened fig tree), the black-crested birds that came stowed
full of potential—mutated germs in the seedpods' husks—in cargo holds

of boats docked in the ship channel, before leaching into the city
like benzene jumping pipes for the gulf. I mean this flood now abated,
yet still as it will be fifty, a hundred years from now, and you, gathered

on what shore you may have found there, you in this echo
I might have detected in pulses under the water's depth,
and—measuring them—have found myself also, does it help

I only wanted so I could have the need? What I denied myself had a border
as elastic as risen dough, the kind that requires a little heat and time
and teams of hungry organisms drunk and belching their conversions.

You are the life in you, like we here are the life in us. I tried spending
the better part of an hour last week casually dredging the net
for a record of the moment the microbiome takes up residence

with our bodies. To complain about the flood as only this flood
and then rue today's temperature is only sticking my hand outside
to get an estimate on the weather. I can report it is uncomfortable,

the air hovering the edges of volcanic breath. If there is a lesson
on how not to worry, it's that you're not stuck only being one thing,
the multitudes in me and the multitudes in you. When ice-melt

exposes the bottle brought aboard the ship suspended on its journey,
whoever finds it might carry gratefully across their lips
these agents of the loop now circling through us.

from *Kenyon Review*

The Seeds

◇　◇　◇

The mouth closes around a word full of O.
Hope: a plea, a sigh, a piece
of enclosed land, a small bounded valley. Also an inlet, a small bay, a haven
in the lake I steer my boat into
      (dropping my good shoes
      and then my feet into the biting
      water) because the water
reminds me of a dance floor. O,
       I'm thirty-four again, in summer,
       giddied by grease smoke and soft serve

from the fast food shacks, my blown-back hair
mimicking the bankside cattails
each time I do a double take
at the drive-in marquee. Each time
I ride a car around the lake

it's an odyssey.
    Did I hope
      like Odysseus or like Penelope?
    I no longer remember the steps

the stranger and I danced
at the party by the water, expecting
what we desired. Sweat darkened my dove-gray
dress, nasturtium petals toppled
through the salad leaves, wavelets
from a storm far offshore

met the black breakwater and surged
                    upward. Like the particular hop
                    in the stomach when I see pews
                    with sky blue cushions stacked
                    in the back of a pickup truck on the highway, or

when we pushed our beds together
in the damp rented room. The lake had already
rolled in our sheets, mildew
marbled the walls with fungal mist.

                    I hoped the storm would stay offshore.
                    I hoped a storm would come in.

It's said there's a wooden chest at the foot of the bed
that a girl should pack with a heart-shaped
stone, a nightgown, and a clump
of forget-me-nots she finds by the stream.
                    Not me. I packed
                    a jar of lake water
and my grandmother's two sets of silver
whose tarnishes clouded the spoons
darker, reminding me to be diligent,
for no woman
                    has swallowed a storm. Along
          with Faith and Love, Hope
is personified as one of the three
heavenly female graces.

Emily Dickinson: "'Hope' is a thing with feathers."
Gertrude Stein: "I hope, I hope and I hope. I hope that I hope and I hope."
Dorothy Wordsworth: "I lingered out of doors in hope of hearing my
          Brothers tread."

Is hope the province of women?

          "As I hope to show": a means
     of arguing gently
in a scholarly essay. The blind peer reviewer
chastised me for using it, correctly assuming

my gender. The water rings on my wooden desk
                              marked pools
                              of thought that I dared
to reign.
          Delete, delete. I erased hope
in order to argue, I presumed,
like a man, offering an analysis not as one of many
provisional approaches to a text
but rather as the only route
to the palace.
                    "I hope all will be well," Ophelia says, but we know
she is doomed when she starts talking
about fennel, columbines, violets and rue.

                    Not a hope in hell, hope against hope, hope for the best.

Ophelia reminds me
                of the mountain laurel
the botanical illustrator placed in a bathtub full of water
to paint branch and bloom undistorted
by gravity, lifelike even
as they died. I've heard
                of a horticulturalist who entered a field
                thinking that whatever he needed
he would find, a method I find irresistible
until I suspect it is only available
to men. The difference between hope
          and entitlement is the difference
                              between imagining how much hay
                              the meadow will bear
                                   and assuming your winter ponies
                                   won't starve.

Gertrude Stein again: "Hope in gates, hope in spoons, hope in doors, hope in
tables, no hope in daintiness and determination. Hope in dates."

Historical hope: on the Internet
you can find a poster of the man who became
president. Red and blue, the word in all caps

like a vine twisting up the stake
of history. A long

time ago. Meanwhile
I circumnavigated a minor lake.
In a car. I was thirty-four
                when I put down the Ziploc of candy
                I'd been surviving on and admitted
                that I was a woman. I stopped hoping
to be a flower girl in a wedding
wearing a daisy crown and scattering petals
from a demolished rose.
              Some say
              that flower girls first
              appeared in weddings
in ancient Rome, carrying bundles
              of wheat. Hope in the body, fertility
              in the field. While I could say
that I hoped to be the symbol
of fertility, hoped to promise
the betrothed a green everlasting earth
as they stepped
into history, I never knew
              who the bride and groom
              would be. I think what I really hoped for
is what I miss hoping for;
to be a wild queen, married
to the flowers and sailing
              through a field
              where fishes swim in the dew.
              I was a child
           until I was thirty-four
       and met the love I'd hoped for. If I hadn't hoped

to be a wild queen, I may not have hoped for a field,
            a small bounded valley
            for my dream daughters
            to drift into
            like two seeds.

How long until winter? Will
the shaggy ponies starve? my real daughters ask me now.
Their questions are the same as mine
                        in that they have no answers,
                                though the lessons of damage
                                are everywhere, as in the parable

of the Texas mountain laurel, whose bright red seeds
                I unwrapped one afternoon
                from a seed pod to place
                in my daughters' hands. The girls were young
                                and tried, by resting
                                the seeds on branches,
                                to put them back
                                in the tree. Unsuccessfully.

That it was too late
                to undo
                what I'd done
                to the tree
        wasn't what I'd hoped to show, though
it was a better lesson, reminding me that only Penelope
                                                can undo the weaving
                                                on the burial shroud.

I hoped like Penelope until I became
a mother. Now I think of hope

as a swing chained to a branch.
It can be used until
                the branch sweeps the ground
                with a shush, shush because
                it cannot bear
        so much weight and still loft through
                        the dream-trafficked air.

I don't care what you say.
A swing may be a child's thing
but the chains

that bind it to the tree
are not.

from *New England Review*

Something to Believe In

◇ ◇ ◇

My two hunting dogs have names, but I rarely use them. As
I go, *they* go: I lead; they follow, the blue-eyed one first, then
the one whose coloring—her coat, not her eyes—I sometimes
call never-again-o-never-this-way-henceforth. Hope, ambition:
these are not their names, though the way they run might suggest
otherwise. Like steam off night-soaked wooden fencing when
the sun first hits it, they rise each morning at my command. Late
in the *Iliad*, Priam the king of Troy predicts his own murder—
correctly, except it won't be by spear, as he imagines, but by
sword thrust. He can see his corpse, sees the dogs he's fed and
trained so patiently pulling the corpse apart. After that, he says,
When they're full, they'll lie in the doorway, they'll lap my blood.
I say: Why shouldn't they? Everywhere, the same people who
mistake obedience for loyalty think somehow loyalty weighs more
than hunger, when it doesn't. At night, when it's time for bed,
we sleep together, the three of us: muscled animal, muscled animal,
muscled animal. The dogs settle to either side of me as if each
were the slightly folded wing of a beast from fable, part power, part
recognition. We breathe in a loose kind of unison. Our breathing
ripples the way oblivion does—routinely, across history's face.

from Poem-a-Day

At Night

◇   ◇   ◇

When did I know that I'd have to carry it around
    in order to have it when I need it, say in a pocket,

the dark itself not dark enough but needing to be
    added to, handful by handful if necessary, until

the way my mother would sit all night in a room
    without the lights, smoking, until she disappeared?

Where would she go, because I would go there.
    In the morning, nothing but a blanket and all her

absence and the feeling in the air of happiness.
    And so much loneliness, a kind of purity of being

and emptiness, no one you are or could ever be,
    my mother like another me in another life, gone

where I will go, night now likely dark enough
    I can be alone as I've never been alone before.

from Poem-a-Day

Fox

◇   ◇   ◇

Kitchen narrow
as a New York

kitchen, shape still
with me thanks to the

plate she threw, it nicked
his cheek, a mark

I tracked beyond
the crayon years

in Ostrava, never
forgetting *ostrá* means

sharp when the noun
is feminine,

and who will now
dig up why she

took up edges, smartest
in school, never topped

on lists surveyed
of boys of the

beautifulest, night
kitchen where she fought

his plan for getting out,
she lost, who loved

to love me most, they'd not
expect a little spy, they had one

time of day to have it out
though I would throw

a plate to make you talk
when baby naps, that's

prime time to write
these fragments out

and then he won
they freed us, bought

a house a Dodge a house
a Buick, I start driving

the Dodge they bought
a Civic, a forest

that was some time
ago, you and I

take trains to this
we rent, I get

to keep that night
kitchen thanks to that

one plate and her ongoing
appetite for seeing

people cut, her news
show is her need

to hurt someone
quite far away,

she's glued to it

from *The American Poetry Review*

Archaeology

◇ ◇ ◇

I went to the basement where my father kept his skulls.
I stood before the metal utility shelves. Skulls to the ceiling.
I looked into the eyeholes. I looked into a cranium's tomahawk hole.
Down there, it was nothing but his lab. I held
those skulls like empty pots. What did I know about Indian pots?
Some days, we went to the bars. I swung my legs from the barstool
and drank my Coke. Some days, he dug the fields.
Then it was skulls in the sink, skulls in the drying rack.
The fields are full of skulls. You have to know where the plows
turn them up. What did I know, then, about digging?
The dark inside the eyeholes. He wrote his notes on them
in indelible ink. 2.7 pounds. 2.5. The fields are full of pots.
It's true. He told me, packing his shovel into the Volkswagen.
What did I know about Indians? He kept a lab in our basement
because the university was too cheap. I went to the basement
where he kept his skulls. I looked into their eyeholes. I loved
their weight, but what did I know? When I lay in bed,
they glowed down there. It was many years ago. I closed my eyes
and the skulls talked in the basement. Indian pots. Teeth.
The noise of sex from his room. At the bars, farmers told him
what their plows turned up. I drank my Cokes. Cheap university
without a decent lab. The skulls spoke a language no one knew.
Look at this, my father said, rinsing another one in the sink.
This one took a bullet to the head. History, then, was silence.
The refrigerator hummed. The skull glowed. He'd scrubbed the soil away.

from *Cherry Tree*

A Partial History

◊ ◊ ◊

Long after I stopped participating

Those images pursued me

I found myself turning from them

Even in the small light before dawn

To meet the face of my own body

Still taut and strong, almost too

Strong a house for so much shame

Not mine alone but also yours

And my brother's, lots of people's,

I know it was irrational, for whom I saw

Myself responsible and to whom

I wished to remain hospitable.

We had all been pursuing our own

Disintegration for so long by then

That by the time the other side

Began to raise a more coherent

Complaint against us we devolved

With such ease and swiftness it seemed

To alarm even our enemies. By then

Many of us had succumbed to quivering

Idiocy while others drew vitality from new

Careers as public scolds. Behind these

Middle-management professors were at pains

To display their faultless views lest they too

Find censure, infamy, unemployment and death

At the hands of an enraged public

Individuals in such pain and torment

And such confusion hardly anyone dared

Ask more of them than that they not shoot

And in fact many of us willed them to shoot

And some of us were the shooters

And shoot we did, and got us square

In the heart and in the face, which anyway

We had been preparing these long years

For bullets and explosions and whatever

Else. A vast unpaid army

Of self-destructors, false comrades, impotent

Brainiacs who wished to appear to be kind

Everything we did for our government

And the corporations that served it we did for free

In exchange for the privilege of watching one

Another break down. Sometimes we were the ones

Doing the breaking. We would comfort one another

Afterward, congratulating each other on the fortitude

It took to display such vulnerability. The demonstration

Of an infirmity followed by a self-justificatory recuperation

Of our own means and our own ends, in short, of ourselves

And our respect for ourselves—this amounted to the dominant

Rhetoric of the age, which some called sharing, which partook

Of modes of oratory and of polemic, of intimate

Journals and of statements from on high issued by public

Figures, whom at one time or another we all mistook ourselves for.

Anyway it wasn't working. None of it was working.

Not our ostentation and not the uses we put our suffering

To, the guilt- and schadenfreude-based attention

We extracted from our *friends* and *followers*, and even the passing

Sensation of true sincerity, of actual truth, quickly emulsified

Into the great and the terrible metastasizing whole.

To the point it began to seem wisest to publish only

Within the confines of our own flesh, but our interiors

Had their biometrics too, and were functions not only

Of stardust, *the universe* as we now were prone to addressing

The godhead, but also of every mean and median of the selfsame

Vicious culture that drove us to retreat into the jail of our own bones

And the cramped confines of our swollen veins and ducts in the first place

Our skin was the same wall they talked about on the news

And our hearts were the bombs whose threat never withdrew

Images could drop from above like the pendulum in "The Pit

And the Pendulum" or killer drones to shatter the face of our lover

Into contemporaneous pasts, futures, celebrities, and other

Lovers all of whom our attention paid equally in confusion

And longing, and a fleeting sense like passing ghosts

Of a barely-remarked-upon catastrophe that was over

Both before and after it was too late. We were ancient

Creatures, built for love and war. Everything said so

And we could not face how abstract it was all becoming

Because it was also all the opposite of abstract, it *was*

Our flesh, our mother's bloodied forehead

On the floor of Penn Station, and wherever we hid

Our face, *amid a crowd of stars* for example as Yeats

Once put it, and for stars insert celebrities

Or astrology here, your choice, and even when

We closed our eyes, all this was all we looked at

Every day all day. It was all we could see.

We were lost in a language of images.

It was growing difficult to speak. Yet talk

Was everywhere. Some of us still sought

To dominate one another intellectually

Others physically; still others psychically or some

Of all of the above, everything seeming to congeal

Into bad versions of sports by other means

And sports by that time was the only metaphor

Left that could acceptably be applied to anything.

The images gave us no rest yet failed over

And over despite the immensity

Of their realism to describe the world as we really

Knew it, and worse, as it knew us

from *Poetry*

The Poorly Built House

◊   ◊   ◊

Venom's slopped over my heart. The four chambers
scuttle away from one another
fear-addled, like scorpions

who can only be killed by the venom dripping
from the three others' tails.

The venom, the doctors tell me, is water.
I've never felt so simple. Water is breaking my heart.

Its weight will make me beat myself to death.
I spoil my limbs, keeping them rich
in blood at all costs. What choice, then, do I have?

My darling ticklers and kickers
are obedient, they deserve the spoiling.
Even now, they slavishly cooperate,
shriveling to be easier to feed.

But they'll never be small enough
to keep my heart from breaking,
there'll be more water, doctors say, till the roof caves,

the chambers—reserved my whole life
for oozing that blood my muscles love—
will flood suddenly with water:
thin, clear, and cold.

I think my dying has been about my belonging.
My body parts seeking where they belong.
I imagine somewhere, my soul is doing the same.

My hair stinks with sweat,
my nostrils are sour with clouds of blood,
while my hips grow sores crusted over with green, sticky pus.

What, children, was so bad about my order?
The life I picked out for us, with my two eyes and best intentions.

Don't think I don't know why. You brats are tearing me up,
sleeping and screaming in the wrong beds,
because you're crazed by my will,
one in a weak hand, hard to read.

In another world, I was never implanted
with that first cancer, panic—

so I never developed the second cancer, cancer.
In this world we never had to make each other into pills,
or use fevers to keep time.

The air was screwed into our chests
by their growing emptiness.

No horses. Not that we could recognize.
Plant life, just a hard green carpet. Forever. Everywhere.

And if you wanted a ship, too bad, no ship. Or, only ships of moss.
That you ate after. Or that dissolved—

like when a child, a nice, good one,
who makes her bed every morning
and is always back in it at ten o'clock,

fills a forest with war machines,
or lunar landers or dragons. And then leaves,

and, when she thinks back on the camping trip,
remembers only a tent, trail mix, the trees.

from *Parnassus*

CLARE ROSSINI

The Keeper Will Enter
the Cage

◇ ◇ ◇

—headline on a nineteenth-century circus poster

It begins with the two of us locked in a long stare,
The crowd slowly shushing.

It knows what I need.
I feel the battering down of instinct, its and mine, our capitulation looming.

Did that curious book of Darwin
Portend our act? Just as the carnal exorbitance of fucking

Evolved over millennia to the restraint, exquisite, of a kiss, so—
Having whipped the beast's spunk out,

Broken its lunge, rode it
Down to a whimper—I'm free to work my hands

Between its lips, then teeth. Whispering tenderly, I crank the heavy jaws
Open. Then into the vast yeasty maw

Goes the tender planet of my skull,
My indelicate philosophy, the memory of the trapeze girl last night,

Her pale thighs, her quick bright yelps of what
I assumed was joy.

Queen Victoria came to watch the act six times.
SIX TIMES! the papers crowed.

Her handmaids fanning as she fingered her necklace of polished stag's teeth.
What did my act awaken

In the mordant empire of her heart, beneath her brocade seething
With South Sea pearls?

Now, face suspended an inch above the lion's lacerating tongue, my eyes
Squeezed shut, I count to five.

Duck back into the brilliant light of afternoon, the crowd
Stomping and whistling in the muddy yard,

The beast making low, pained mewling sounds as we behold one another, both
Ravaged by what I had done.

from *Parnassus*

American Cockroach

◇ ◇ ◇

When the American cockroach lands
on its back trying to
flick the glorious
wasp off that moves like the hybrid of green tin
and blue glass, gem-
tragic cerulean

task, finite and fathomable as
a photoshopped sea, the
plan is already
in full swing: into the neurotransmitter-
primeval that
drives the bidding of the

now upended resolute legs of
cockroach American—
six times the size of
the wasp, and the color of a bottle of
Budweiser—thrusts
the neurosurgical

stinger, the accuracy of which
is neither hate nor love
but the beginning
of the brief paralysis in which she needs
to suspend the
roach so, unimpeded,

she can target a second cockroach
ground zero in its roach-
ancient cockroach head.
Do not fear mystery over precision.
That's the mistake
of children in bed whose

abstract suspicions are dismissed. There
was a jewel. Its name
is wasp. She flies off
now to construct a specific nest. Do you
think the roach is
dead? There it stands doing

nothing when the wasp returns drained
from stinging, which you know
kills dead the honey
bees you dreamed of as a girl that prompted you
to pose your first
questions to self as to

sacrifice and valor—and so
weary now, drags herself
toward the roach, who makes
no move to defend itself, and bites off just
one of the crisp
antennae who among

us has not been queried by—as
I was once from a crack
in a cabinet
in a kitchen I was sharing with a friend
whose ex I should
not have slept with. Well, that

was unexpected. I haven't
thought that trespass through in
a long time. Poems
are as good a place for the past as the grass

is for the wasp,
whose iridescent face

shines as she snaps the antennae
off the cockroach and laps
up the blood drink like
the wasp goddess taught her in the vision whose
street name, instinct,
oversimplifies how

satisfying I'm finding it
to say cock as often
as I have had the
occasion to here; American cock, in
particular.
I have good instincts. I

always have. People never shock
me, but I love to be
taken by surprise
by loyalty and candor. How I want the
wasp to mount and
ride the American

cockroach now, but it will have to
do to see the wasp use
the one antenna
the roach has left as a rein to steer it to
the nest she made
it, as a dutiful

stallion of apocalypse is
gently led back to its
stall in hell. Yes, it
will have to do, for now, having soul-hacked the
American
cockroach with a sting to

the brain so precise as to make
the roach stop roach-ident-

ifying and give
itself, body and force, zombie host to the
wasp egg the wasp
is laying inside it,

siblingless, starving-born hatchling
emerging in a few
weeks' time by eating
itself out of the moist gut of the living
roach, who was led,
as I said, not ridden

by the wasp—no riding crop, no
matriarch giddyup,
just a groom and a
walk, and a nest and an egg, and a roach called
cock. It is, it
is, it is enough, but

this is evolution and we've
already come this far.

from *The New Yorker*

Shainadas

◇ ◇ ◇

Ese Louie ...
Chale, call me "Diamonds," man!
——José Montoya

He shined shoes
as a boy for movie money,
& I imagined how

a shinebox might fit
under the theater's seat
the way it fit decades

later when I saw it
in that dark beneath
my grandparent's old,

sunken spring-bed.
Later bulldozed,
the Phoenix theater

must have looked
like those pre-war
cinemas mostly lost

now but documented
in the photographs
of Hiroshi Sugimoto——

for which the artist
placed his large
format camera

in the last rows
of spring-shut seats
below ornate

wall-carvings
& baroque sconces
where he then

left the camera's
aperture open
for a full feature.

It is what we see
of stars—all endings
& untouchable

beginnings: images,
characters, & plot
gone & only white

light left. The cedar box
housing brushes,
rags, & tins of polish

had its hinged latch
& the handle that
also cradled a shoe.

My foot's never
touched it, but I wonder
which brush inside

might brush back,
against the grain,
one of those photos

to extend the wet
finger of projection
over a boy, who looks

up toward the screen
like he looked
up from a shine.

Or is the figure
to borrow from that
other invention?

Could I carve open
a pinhole in the shinebox
for its storehouse

of inverted images?
—as if revolutions were that
simple an apparatus

of optics to have
the shiner ascend there
to what shines.

from *Poetry Northwest*

Dysphonia

◇ ◇ ◇

I suppose the thrushes skittering about the yard
Steeped in lilac in ways we calmly despise
Also contain wet lingual rashes laid like cards
Interstitially arranged & with surprise,

By which I mean I'm sorry, too, father, you really are
Losing your mind. We both seek out
Odd term lexicons, knick-knacks to scar
Basic emotions, as if *fibrosis* will somehow

Achieve complex harmony & crystal accuracy.
I watched you slice tomatoes at the pace of . . .
At the pace of . . . I look out the window, trees,
Aspens, pitifully gathered. Oh okay, bradykinesia.

I cut them for you, you turn on Jethro Tull.
Something about innovation, flutes, rock, medi-
Eval performances with Shakespearean skulls—
I've never seen a body perform slow-diving

Its own death before. You leave the room
To weep, reminding me I've never seen you cry
Before. Pathogenesis is nonetheless a spoonful
Of beginning, idiopathic maps, a jittery

Herd &c.—Sure, I'll throw in the roast.
You say, It's multiple system atrophy, you see?
We walk Chloe, talk about the Pacific Coast,
Parkland, Washington, about the disease,

How it makes roads between mind & body
Troublingly clear. Dopaminergic systems spit
Complex happy while the basal ganglia sees
Neural loss as one does loss itself—gilt

Beginnings, youth, debauchery, then sobriety,
Guilt, wasted days, years, ruined marriages,
Fealties turned faulty, the cumulonimbi
Wholly imaginary—the crashed carriage.

Pull out the roast! I have to *tell* my legs to move
In order to walk, my voice . . . *dysphonia*.
We watch hockey, which is our proven
Bond. Their bodies carve gracefully on ice.

from *New England Review*

Sprang

◊ ◊ ◊

1 Winter Stars

You will never forget corpses wrapped in flames—
at dusk, you watched a congregation of crows

gather in the orchard and sway on branches;
in the dawn light, a rabbit moves and stops,

moves and stops along the grass; and as
you pull a newspaper out of a box, glance

at the headlines, you feel the dew on grass
as the gleam of fading stars: yesterday you met

a body shop owner whose father was arrested,
imprisoned, and tortured in Chile, heard

how men were scalded to death in boiling water;
and, as the angle of sunlight shifts, you feel

a seasonal tilt into winter with its expanse
of stars—candles flickering down the Ganges,

where you light a candle on a leaf and set it
flickering, downstream, into darkness—

dozens of tiny flames flickering into darkness—
then you gaze at fires erupting along the shore.

2   Hole

No sharp-shinned hawk perches
on the roof rack of his car and scans
for songbirds; the reddening ivy
along a stone wall deepens in hue;
when he picks a sun-gold tomato
in the garden and savors
the burst in his mouth, he catches
a mock orange spray in the air;
and as he relights the pilot
to a water heater, checks thermostats,
the sound of water at a fountain
is prayer; earlier in the summer,
he watched a hummingbird land,
sip water, and douse its wings,
but, now, a widening hole gnaws
at that time; and, glancing
at a spotted-towhee nest on a lintel,
he knows how hunting chanterelles
at the ski basin and savoring
them at dinner is light-years away.

3   Talisman

Quetzal: you write
        the word on a sheet of paper
                then erase it;

each word, a talisman,
        leaves a track: a magpie
                struts across a portal

and vanishes from sight;
        when you bite into sea urchin,
                ocean currents burst

in your mouth; and when
        you turn, view the white shutters
                to the house,

up the canyon, a rainbow
        arcs into clouds;
                expectancies, fears, yearnings—

hardly bits of colored glass
        revolving in a kaleidoscope—
                mist rising from a hot spring

along a river: suddenly
        you are walking toward Trinity Site
                searching for glass

and counting minutes
        of exposure under the sun;
                suddenly small things ignite.

He slips on ice near a mailbox—

no gemsbok leaps across the road—

a singer tapped an eagle feather on his shoulders—

women washed indigo-dyed yarn in this river, but today gallium and
   germanium particles are washed downstream—

once they dynamited dikes to slow advancing troops—

picking psilocybin mushrooms and hearing cowbells in the mist—

as a child, he was tied to a sheep and escaped marauding soldiers—

an apple blossom opens to five petals—

as he hikes up a switchback, he remembers undressing her—

from the train window, he saw they were on ladders cutting fruit off cacti—

in the desert, a crater of radioactive glass—

assembling shards, he starts to repair a gray bowl with gold lacquer—

they ate psilocybin mushrooms, gazed at the pond, undressed—

hunting a turkey in the brush, he stops—

from the ponderosa pines: *whoo-ah, whoo whoo whoo—*

5   Yellow Lightning

In the 5 a.m. dark, a car with bright lights
and hazard lights blinking drives directly at me;
veering across the yellow lines, I pass by it

and exhale: amethyst crystals accrete
on a string: I will live to see pear
blossoms in the orchard, red-winged black-

birds nesting in the cattails; I love the sighs
you make when you let go—my teeth gripping
your earlobe—pearls of air rising through water—

and as a white moon rising over a canyon
casts pine shadows to the ground, gratitude
rivers through me: sharpened to starlight,

I make our bed and find your crystal
between the sheets; and when I part the curtains,
daylight's a strobe of yellow lightning.

6   Red-Ruffed Lemur

You locate a spotted-towhee nest on a beam,
peony shoots rising out of the earth, but a pang
surges in your blood with each systole—
though spring emerges, the forsythia eludes you—
in a coffee shop, a homeless man gathers
a Chinese magazine and two laundered towels
in a clear plastic bag, mutters "Metro,"
and heads out the door—a bird trills
in the blue spruce, but when it stops, the silence
is water running out of thawing glacial ice;
and you mix cement in a wheelbarrow,
haul it, in a bucket, up a ladder to a man
on a rooftop plastering a parapet—cherry buds
unfurl along a tidal basin—a red-ruffed
lemur squints out of a cage at human faces,
shudders, and scurries back into a hole—
and you surge at what's enfolded in this world:

7 This Is the Writing, the Speaking of the Dream

Red bougainvillea blooming against the glass—

she likes it when he pulls her to him—

once you saw murres crowding the cliffs of an arctic island—

thousands of blue-black mussels, exposed and gripping rocks at low tide—

he runs his fingers between her toes—

light reflecting off snow dazzles their eyes—

a tiger shark prowls along the shoreline for turtles—

an aspen leaf drops into a creek—

when he tugs the roots of her hair, he begins to tiger—

this is the writing, the speaking of the dream—

no one knows why ten thousands of murres are dying—

he hungers for sunlight to slant along their bodies on a Molokai slope—

sunlight streams as gold-flecked koi roil the waters and churn—

they roil the waters and churn—

killer whales move through Prince William Sound—

8   Net Light

Poised on a bridge, streetlights
on either shore, a man puts
a saxophone to his lips, coins
in an upturned cap, and a carousel

in a piazza begins to turn:
where are the gates to paradise?
A woman leans over an outstretched
paper cup—leather workers sew

under lamps: a belt, wallet, purse—
leather dyed maroon, beige, black—
workers from Seoul, Lagos, Singapore—
a fresco on a church wall depicts

the death of a saint: a friar raises
both hands in the air—on an airplane,
a clot forms in a woman's leg
and starts to travel toward her heart—

a string of notes riffles the water;
and, as the clot lodges, at a market
near lapping waves, men unload
sardines in a burst of argentine light.

9 Sprang

Before tracking pods of killer whales
in Prince William Sound, she reads a poem

on deck to start each day. In solstice light,
a moose lumbers across a driveway; I mark

orange and purple sea stars exposed at low tide,
the entrance to an octopus den. Astronomers

have observed two black holes colliding;
and, though the waves support relativity,

we need no equation to feel the sprang of space
and time. A marine biologist gives everything

away, weaves her coffin out of alder branches,
lines it with leaves; a carpenter saws kiln-

dried planks to refurbish a porch; I peruse
the tips of honeycrisp apples we planted

last fall, and, though no blossoming appears,
the air is rife with it; the underground

stirs, and I can only describe it by saying
invisible deer move through an orchard in bloom.

from *Mānoa*

The Prayer

◇　◇　◇

My dog came back from the woods smelling of skunk, so I gave him a good wash in the tub outside and things were better. We took a walk down the street and met another dog, a big one. They snarled at one another and then made their peace. After a good walk we turned around and went back home. Robbie, the dog, went to sleep in his corner, and I did some paperwork. I was going along just fine until there was a knock on the door. I answered it and it was my ex-wife. She said she had come for the dog and I said that wasn't in the agreement. She said she had bought the dog and it was hers. I said Robbie loved me. She said a dog doesn't know what love is. "This is the dog's home, his neighborhood," I said. "He'll adapt to his new home in a day," she said. "You don't give this dog real feelings about anything," I said. "He's a dog, for Christ's sake," she said. "He's my dog. He comes when I call him, he sits when I tell him to, he fetches, he sleeps when I sleep. We're like married to each other," I said. "And now he wants to divorce you," she said. "He does not. We're happy together," I said. "Well, we'll be happy together, too," she said. "It would break his heart to leave me," I said. "You don't know what you're talking about," she said. I called Robbie. He didn't come. I called him again. "Where's your dog now?" she said. "I'll get him," I said. I went and looked in the bedroom. He wasn't there. I looked in the study. He wasn't there either. I went in the guest bedroom. He wasn't there. I came back into the living room. "I can't find him," I said. "He's got to be someplace," she said. "You didn't let him out when you came in, did you?" I said. "Definitely not," she said. "Well, I can't find him in the house," I said. "Robbie!" she called, "Robbie!" He wasn't anywhere. "What are we going to do?" I said. "Let's pray," she said. "What?" I said. "Let's pray for Robbie to come back, it can't hurt," she said. "Okay, if you think it might help," I said. We closed our eyes and held hands. "Heavenly Father, please bring our Robbie safely back to us," she said. We opened our eyes and there was a camel standing there. "Oh, no, you've made a mistake," I said. "I didn't make a mistake. God did," she said. "Come here, Robbie," I said. And the huge animal stepped nearer and rubbed his snout on my shoulder just like Robbie always did when he wanted to express his affection for me. "He's half yours," I said.

from *Conduit*

Sitting Isohydric Meditation

◇ ◇ ◇

weather is water
      is one way to think

about the season
      seizing the street tree

another drought year
      measured in questions

I asked the nurses
      who gently strapped me

to the clang & throb
      inside the passing

time the MRI
      ground into windows

the doctor looked through
      to see my future

I sit on the couch
      & watch the sparrows

on the branches pant
      & puff their feathers

a sort of solstice
      truce with the dry heat

moving scorch from edge
        to stem on each leaf

the heat's so quiet
        it's a kind of pain

nothing seems to soothe
        not even his damp

armpit & its scent
        of moss soaked with rain

woody sweet dear
        bacterial earth

mouth my mouth opens
        onto & into

his skin confusing
        outside inside me

when we fuck we go
        deep mammal all fur

& genital scent
        in my beard a soak

of pheromones taut
        swollen erectile

tissue & the swoon
        of adrenaline

a chemical world
        that feels insular

but is immersed in
        stimulus the way

a magnetic field
  held my prone body

whose protons aligned
  their axes & flipped

their spins to allow
  radio waves

through flesh made newly
  resonant I felt

removed from the world
  & cocooned in sound

while the protons slowed
  & their spins flipped back

radio signals
  that rendered image

vertebral detail
  so precise it hurt

to look at the bones
  as the doctor talked

drought's about being
  porous & storing

water if you can't
  travel to get it

so some tree species
  close their stomata

& wait for water
  the way maples do

dying slowly from
        edges to center

as a stress response
        it's a real gamble

to shut yourself up
        inside of yourself

if I could I would
        stay as open as

his face when I sit
        on his cock & he

holds my hips & tilts
        himself up deeper

injury insists
        it remain hidden

& grows its quota
        of pain from the bones

the doctor showed me
        calcifications

white as dry lichen
        leaching life from

a lip of granite
        how to keep going

into the quotient
        of future the bones

divide inside me
        the incurable

instance a given
     faultless or at fault

I remain hidden
     how to keep going

from *New England Review*

I Am a Father Now

◇ ◇ ◇

I am a father now, an unprecedented thing
I never was before and have always been,
preparing, preparing since I was born a father's son,
and not a mother's daughter. Plus I married a daughter's
mother, little did I know. But how could I?
It had only been a moment since I arrived—
I was barely conceived on one of time's
unremembered nights, and suddenly I woke
with a child crying in each ear, these years
like the coils of a patient snake that has lovingly
nibbled and swallowed me countlessly.
I am diminished to a great height, the ceiling
of the world tickling the tips of my lost hairs.
I loom like the moon over two baby baboons,
my helpless, hopeful hobbits, one for each
leaden eye. I might be just like my father's
father for all I know. I could be the bearer
of my mother's father's nose, and look
what I've done with it, seat of my driving glasses.
I'm the lover, quietly, furtively, of the bearer
of my daughter and son—the fever of our sex
shakes the house we uphold, but let's not wake
the children here or next door or next door to that.
Or let's wake them up and play with them now
while no one's looking, for joy is always
our secret, the secret of this hurried, harried life
without horses. I sleep when I can, and I can't die.
I have never been as mortal as now. I bend low,
my back aching and breaking under grateful weight.

No matter—I'll grow another. I have my children
to thank for my bending body, which is born
a hundred times each day, dying every breath.

from *Conduit*

LYNNE THOMPSON

She talk like this 'cause me Mum born elsewhere, say

◊   ◊   ◊

Ackee   and talk funny—make things up,
                         but say apples, apricot—then say
                         ackee—both fruit and juice make
                         you feel good from the

Beginning   when she insulted Episcopalian
                         Jesus, singing (top of her lungs)
                         big-inning like a good

Caribbean—   or potato or po-tay-toe to a fool
                         who say Caribbean—she laugh—
                         Cari-bee-an . . . she say

Dasheen: *US got greens*, but me mum got
                         something else like

Egret   is same   yes   but

Fiddle-faddle   she never said, afraid of the

Government   & warned: *enunciate the first* n
                         like you got good schoolin' not

Hard knocks,   as in school of—

[is this   making any sense?] Are you hungry for

jumbee soursop?   foul-smelling, bitter,
                      good for make you suffer and

keep quiet   (this has nothing to do with mum being
                      from Bequia [she say *Beck*-way]) she say

Legoland?   but her mouth waterin' for
                      leg of lamb and

money   *never got enough where you from and*

Nurdle   as in a game of cricket when
                      the batsman nudges the ball
                      around and into a purée of

onions—   *never make a meal without 'em,*

Pamela,   (my 1st name she never call me) like I'm

Queer   you mean like the guy who lived
                      in the house behind ours? He drink

Rum   then

Sweets   *The sound when suck*
                      air through teeth like
                      low-class people from

Trinidad . . .   (sotto voce) *your father's people,*
                      not sweet, sail from there to

187

USA	then again, mum was never truly
	n a t u r a l i z e d like a
Vegeee-tuble	spinach, peas, or beet soup
	causing—*ha!*—
wee wee	but no one say this when
	referring to piss & need some
X-rays	that don't show the way to float on a
Yah-chit *or* yacht	& make we laugh when mum butcher
	English except she remembers she's a
Zebra	that is same as you say when you
	mix the black & white—

from *Pleiades*

MATTHEW THORBURN

The Stag

◇　◇　◇

—*after Gerhard Richter's* Stag (Hirsch),
oil on canvas, 1963

I couldn't see a way out
for him the woods
too tangled those arrowing
branches pinned him in
one broad trunk weighed

him down no break
in sight no light shafting
through and what did you do
I lay still among the bodies
and how did you live

I played dead as the dead
grew cold all night
and why didn't you scream
I did scream down
in the dark I kept it locked

behind my teeth and why
did you close your eyes
so I could see the stag instead
his head turned to me
I watched until he blurred

189

away into pale gray light
and why tell us this
because I've grown old because
my punishment for living
is to keep living.

from *Cave Wall*

Isfahan, 2010

◇　◇　◇

—for Maman joon and Baba joon and the Kooye Emam view

Back bent with bones emptied, my grandmother wants to know
what to fix me before the flight, in the kitchen patterned
with seared circles from stove-licked pots sitting too long on carpet.
Something, *maman*, she says, you can't find there; this early when
Isfahan morning is the color of sand and barley, when the sun
is teasing the August scape, a leftover breeze from last night
must be caught before afternoon heat devours it; already I hear
skewers clatter over someone's fire, the rapid knife press to parsley
stems, coriander, and dill; by now I can name herbs by the essence
of each bouquet. Only a short while ago did the rooster crow,
did the echo from high towers awaken the god in the sleepers,
but the dried skin of cardamom cracked in the steam of black tea
roused the pious first, and Hayedeh's pining voice streams from a neighbor's
home, strikes my gut before my ears, a farewell song to her homeland;
I remember she is buried in Los Angeles. And across this window,
the yard stirs with the rush of a hose, the bristle scratch
of sweepers in the space where my mother in school uniform once
played with classmates. On the sidewalk, a young boy slings
over his arm *sangak* loaves, toasted and dimpled by flicked stones.
Here, they tell me they know I eat fancy, *Amrikayee*, with your forever
selection of breads, tell me they know I prefer high-rises, right-angled
streets, not this city of vaulted arches, of ancient turquoise framing
the alphabet script that traveled across empires to reach these walls.
And though I have yet to respond, my grandmother grates shallots,
the aroma of which I know will stay stubborn beneath her nails,
will cling to crimson cushions and rugs like rosewater, like yogurt

with peeled cucumbers—I wish this brew would not glide like perfume,
the scent mix I cannot inhale again, and even if a whiff of it sneaks
to New York, I wouldn't know how to seal it, like the urban clamor
beyond the kitchen, the motorcycle buzz and copper tray clang
in locked shops, or the river drying, the quiet haze that fogs horizon
mountains, pales the honeycomb nooks of a past glory; each movement
is a crawling melody where the Wi-Fi is still spotty, public transit still
in progress, and above all, none of this translates into either language,
the yearning for a space at least somewhere in between, but
the Atlantic is no anchor for this, the ocean does not house permanent
residents, drowns those who weren't happy with any piece of ground
to keep their feet rooted. And with no direct airline to fly us
immediately between hemispheres, forgetting and longing become
equally easy—the price paid when you and your mother are born
in different countries. But for now, I know that later, after midnight,
my grandfather will drive me two hours to the airport, pack the seats
with aunts and cousins, messages to deliver, bury his old, tearful eyes
in the shuffle of my suitcases. And before I am lifted back
into a sapphire sky that seats me above a million lights,
each bearing the name of a paradise garden, a woman will stamp
my passport goodbye. She will tell me to come back again and
when she says my name, she does not skip over the *H*, extends it
instead, and I am full with the sound this makes, that of a deep breath
pulled from the cellar of her lungs, and for a second, I find home in the air
held in this stranger's mouth; something, *maman joon*, I can't find there.

from *Michigan Quarterly Review*

Recessional

◇ ◇ ◇

After the cake—
five-tiered, chocolate ganache, complete
with actual orchids
atop the fondant—the long buildup
to the last

last song, the father
of the bride slumped—one
too many courtyard cocktails—
in his chair, and after the pink
jasmine, andromeda, the dusty

garden roses softening
in a cut-glass vase in a corner
of the ballroom. After
pates de fruits, lemon tartlets.
After the toasts.

After the dinner served alfresco,
underneath tree boughs
and bistro lights. After the three-piece band
has exhausted
its covers,

the bride,
in her fitted-bodice blush
pink gown,
declares their exit. The fireworks write
their postscript across the sky

and not one of us thinks what we look like
            from above, nor of
the eleven-vehicle wedding procession
                        delivering the newlyweds
            to the groom's remote village.

                    A pilotless plane
            pauses. One man looks up.
We know the rest from headlines.
                    How the attendants
            leapt from their cars before

                        they caught fire.
Broken glass. Scraps of hot metal
            striking the bride's face. Scorched
            trucks and sandals left
scattered on the road. Seconds later

            the echo beyond
                        the stone-built houses, the riverbed,
the highlands. Yes, one man,
                        the article says, looked up
            when the familiar hum

            of the drone—this
is what the sky now sounds like—
                        stopped. Imagine,
though, the moment before. The bride's hand
            on her mother's wet cheek.

Keep the groom's son
                        breathing, the truck
            intact. Poetry says, there is eternity
                in the moment.
            But as we with our sparklers

            light the path for our
new couple to their limousine
            door, as they raise the window

behind which they will become
               invisible,

          we see only ourselves. "Our art,"
               wrote Petrarch,
"is that which makes men immortal
               through fame." Turning back
to gather our summer shawls and high heels

          from the dance floor,
we recount, already, the day. The bride's smart
               braids. The ribbon
holding each cloth napkin. The balloons
               rising away

          from the city. What love poem
could be written when men can no longer
               look up?
In their thank you notes—
               calligraphed perfectly

in plum ink—the bride and groom include
          a candid photograph for each
attendee. In the moment,
          we didn't even know
                    we were touching.

          from *Pleiades*

Samson, 1674

◊   ◊   ◊

(for John Milton)

Their theaters cackle and bray, their carriages
clutter the streets: cockades, torches, liveries
clash. Philistine hearts
jocund and sublime, they smear their deals

gold on columns and cornices. Temples fume
with burning fat. The choicest girls
parade with kohl-ringed eyes and spangled thighs.
Let the poor creep into shadows: they offend.

The prisons teem. And one old man
sits in his doorway in a loose gray coat
letting sunlight lay its palms on his sightless eyes.
He's seen too much. Kingdoms askew,

skies collapsing, idols crammed back into shrines.
Let the mad cavalcade pass by.
There's a kind of defeat that resembles victory.
There's a temple raised up only in the mind

and another to be pulled down
in dream, arms wrapped around massive pillars
to tug and shatter the roof on guzzling lords.
Not by his arms, not by his gouty hands.

But the phoenix spark sleeps in ash.

from *The Paris Review*

Machinery

◊　◊　◊

My father loved every kind of machinery,
relished bearings, splines, windings, and cogs,
loved the tolerances between moving parts
and the parts that moved the parts,
the many separate machines of machinery.
Loved the punch, the awl, the ratchet, the pawl.
In-feed and out-feed rollers of the thickness planer,
its cutter head and cutters. The barrel and belt sanders,
the auger, capstan, windlass, and magneto.
Such a beautiful vocabulary in his work, words
he knew even if often he did not know
how they were spelled. Seals, risers, armatures.
Claw, ball-peen, sledge, dead-blow, mallet,
hammers all. Butt, mitered, half-lap,
tongue and groove; mortise and tenon,
biscuit, rabbet, dovetail, and box: all joints.
"A poem is a small (or large) machine
made of words," said William Carlos Williams.
"To build the machine that makes the machine,"
said Elon Musk. Once my father repaired
a broken harpsichord but could not make it sing.
The chock, the bore, the chisel. He could hang a door,
rebuild an engine. Cylinders, pistons, and rings.
Shafts, crank and cam. Hand-cut notches
where the hinges sat. He loved the primary feathers
on the wings of a duck, extended and catching air,
catching also the tops of the white-cap waves
when it landed. Rods, valves, risers, and seals.
Ailerons and flaps, yaw control in the tail.

Machinery, machinery, machinery, machinery.
Four syllables in two iambic feet. A soft pulse.
Once I told him what Williams said,
he approached what I made with deeper interest
but no more understanding in the end.
The question he did not ask, that would have
embarrassed him to ask, the question I knew
he wanted to ask, the one I was too embarrassed
to ask for him, was "What does it do?"
Eventually the machine his body was was broken,
and now it is gone, and the mechanically inclined
machine in his head is also gone,
and most of his tools, the machines that made
the machines, are gone too, but for a few
I have kept in remembrance. A fine wood plane
but not the thickness planer, which I would not know
how to use. A variety of clamps I use to clamp
things-needing-clamping clamped. Frost said
"poetry is the sort of thing poets write." My father
thought it was the sort of thing I wrote,
but what mattered to him was what it did.
And what does it do? A widget that resists
conclusions. A crank that turns a wheel
that turns. A declaration of truth
by a human being running at full speed
in a race with no one, toward nowhere
except away from the beginning and toward arrival.
Once my father watched the snow
and noted how landing on the earth it melted.
He said, "It's snow that doesn't know it's rain."

from *The Georgia Review*

Reading Not Reading

◊   ◊   ◊

Out loud we
      are
a silence, isn't

      it thought,
conglomerate
purpose, the old

head
considering
      what to say;

ought one
      be
      bound

to it—
      but I can't
be thinking

like this I am
instead
      reading,

am
trying
      to read

against
      this thought
of what to say,

to be
      bound to,
to say and be

bound to it,
      but not even
that, not the reading,

not the
thought of
      what to say

      but a vision, one
that moves,
      it moves

      like a car
or a train
      or just like

light—
you and I
      are intimate—

I read about
      the forest
with you nearby

I read and
you are
      nearby,

moving, the vision,
it is a memory
      of the big lake

and the city,
            a memory
of the mornings

every morning
            the look of the lake
past the park

and the bike path,
            you would know
what I mean

if I said this
            to you, if you
read this now, but I

                        don't
show it, you are nearby,
the memory runs, it runs

like writing runs,
            an executable,
I am reading but I am not

            reading, you are
nearby (we are
on a beach, a stony beach,

there are gulls,
children
            flying kites)

I should mention
            the forest is soft,
in this reading, they are

by a stream,
pausing,
attending to themselves,

in the midst
of a
       plan, (what

to say
and be
       bound by?)

       but I am
not reading, you are
nearby,

here, I think
       is how to
say it.

from *Poetry Northwest*

JOHN YAU

The President's Telegram

◇   ◇   ◇

No child or teacher should ever feel terrible in an American school
My prayers should feel safe to the victims of a terrible child
My condolences to the families of anyone else
Should anyone feel unsafe in school, my condolences
Should anyone feel unsafe in a family, my prayers
Should anyone else ever feel unsafe, my prayers and condolences
Should my prayers feel unsafe, my condolences to the terrible school
Unsafe child and unsafe teacher feel my prayers

from *The Massachusetts Review*

Opioid, Alcohol, Despair

◇ ◇ ◇

1-

Feel for your lying there, how could I fail
   a man lying there poor guy, lies there; there's—
     nowhere to go. He can barely lift his limbs.
Moreover his core, contracted—you can't see it
   has fallen, into the asphalt, X marked there
    —his early burial—there? Though
some nights (I would think) his brain

                      —awakens—
   to a sound. Of commiseration.
     Destination. As to a hymn a moment
stretching—
   itself, though not a mirror cracking: faces
    in a progression of shame, of the same self-
loathing, how could it not now *be him* & I know
   it's wrong to stare at blank gaze. Worse, to shut out
    the gaze. Maybe next time I might not pass on
to the other side; might even give him a five
   dollar bill or an apple or a handful of quarters,
   dimes (how could he buy vodka with that?)
so that he can sleep, piss not in public maybe
   next time, throw in a throw-blanket too so that I

                    can sleep, walk on.

2-

      And this is the way it happens some wintry
descent out of the blue to below-freeze weather
      wheezes a man asleep on a mat in a tunnel in Philly
        need not be hail sleet snow could be an alley sunny
LA or right in the heart of Silicon Valley the story
      has to meet suffering. Where there is a void someone
        fills it. Perhaps the poet he, a stand-in—philosophically
in blue key, the vowels dusty & mauve/ The man
      can't move! past—childhood
                            —trauma—after trauma.
      The blows. The feeling
—of superfluous. Suicide in the bottle
      of Tylenol, gin. Oxycodone. Our anti-hero or
        heroine: in the tunneled needle. The drug—
is not the problem. Something in the weariness
      in his bones. Was it the father's?/can't condone can't
      undone. A vortex of smoke. Evaporations really

of all he had or ever wanted to have ambition a job his wife
      suddenly left him, I'm guessing.

3-

      Another version, how it all began, junior high, a
birthday present given to him for high,
      for vice: black tar shimmerings in heat, for
        inhalation; fine white powder uncut
with sugar, cocaine. Which he took for—antidote
—to suffocation. Ennui. So easy . . . the easing into
      the tied-off vein. Into fantastic shapes, his mind a jungle
warped: into spirals. Blood fell from the sky. Boiled in the
—body *here your body*; *well-being*—one
                         rush . . . then another
      & what follows not just in a more acute
crisis—
      than we knew, the scale & darkness, phosphorous
      —had he known? Or had it been all along—indifference,

let's say, to life? To the heart's simplicity
    to pain? A withdrawal & nothingness? And now
        slumped against a wall without proper shoes,
                                            —no data—
having walked pawn shops brown
    newspapers trash-blown made up of cut-out
        aspiration—or desperation, & rain
drumming on the roofs of cars . . .

4-

And the sense of loss after loss, sequences—
        what do we say: a disease? All those studies
in brain science MRI
                            —darkness—whole cities
    in peril: silent schizophrenias wandering
        street corners; lit up: the brain's reds
& yellows & we stand there in awe—starting
    to see: the brain's (struggling) changes
        in bright yellows, greens. Blues & purples. And
who will be found—awakening
—as from a drugged mind as from dream-
    sequences—we who stand there still
—still staring at consequences staring
                            —in our sterile, white coats?

                from *Kenyon Review*

Study of Two Figures
(Pasiphaë/Sado)

◇   ◇   ◇

One figure is female, the other is male.

Both are contained.

One figure is mythical, the other historical.

To the extent that one can be said to have existed at all, they occupy different millennia, different continents.

But, to the extent that one can be said to have existed at all, both figures are considered Asian—one from Colchis, one from Korea.

To mention the Asianness of the figures creates a "racial marker" in the poem.

This means that the poem can no longer pass as a white poem, that different people can be expected to read the poem, that they can be expected to read the poem in different ways.

To mention the Asianness of the figures is also to mention, by implication, the Asianness of the poet.

Revealing a racial marker in a poem is like revealing a gun in a story or like revealing a nipple in a dance.

After such a revelation, the poem is *about* race, the story is *about* the gun, the dance is *about* the body of the dancer—it is no longer considered a dance at all and is subject to regulation.

Topics that have this gravitational quality of *about*ness are known as "hot button" topics, such as race, violence, or sex.

"Hot button" is a marketing term, coined by Walter Kiechel III, in a September 1978 issue of *Fortune* magazine.

The term evokes laboratory animals and refers to consumer desires that need to be slaked.

The term "hot button" suggests not only the slaking of such desires but also a shock or punishment for having acted on those desires, a deterrent to further actions pursuing such desires, and by extension, a deterrent to desire itself.

Violence and sex are examples of desires and can be satisfied, punished, and deterred.

Race is not usually considered an example of desire.

Both the female and the male figures are able to articulate their desires with an unusual degree of candor and specificity.

Both are responsible for many sexual deaths.

The male figure says, "When anger grips me, I cannot contain myself. Only after I kill something—a person, perhaps an animal, even a chicken—can I calm down. . . . I am sad that Your Majesty does not love me and terrified when you criticize me. All this turns to anger." "Your Majesty," here, refers to the king, his father.

The female figure is never directly quoted, but Pseudo-Apollodorus writes that she casts a spell upon the king her husband so that when he has sex with another woman, he ejaculates wild creatures into the woman's vagina, thereby killing her. Although the punishment is enacted on the body of the woman, this punishment is meant to deter the king from slaking his desires.

Both figures, royal themselves, are angry at the king, but neither attempts to kill the king—which would be political. Instead they displace this anger onto other unnamed deaths, which are considered sexual but not political.

Both figures have spouses known for strategy, for self-preservation in politically tumultuous times, times of many unnamed deaths.

Both figures are counterfoils to their strategizing spouses, figures of excessive desire, requiring containment.

Both containers are wooden.

Both containers are camouflaged with a soft, yielding substance—one with grass, one with fur.

Both containers are ingenious solutions to seemingly intractable problems.

One problem is political. One problem is sexual.

They are both the same problem.

They have the same solution.

The male figure waits in the container for death to come. He waits for eight days. His son will live. This ensures the succession, the frictionless transfer of power.

The female figure waits in the container for the generation of a life. We do not know how long she waits. Her son will die, after waiting in his own wooden container. This ensures the succession, the frictionless transfer of power.

There are many artistic representations of both containers.

The male figure's container is blockish, unadorned, a household object of standard size and quotidian function. Tourists climb into it and pose for photos, post them online. The cramped position of their bodies generates a combination of horror and glee. This, in turn, creates discomfort, the recognition that horror and glee should not be combined, that such a combination is taboo.

The female figure's container is customized, lushly contoured. Its contours are excessively articulated to the same degree that her desire is excessively articulated. Artists depict the container in cutaway view, revealing the female figure within, awaiting the wild creature. The abject position of the female figure—on all fours, pressing her genitalia back against the hollow cow's genitalia—generates a combination of lust and revenge. This, in turn, creates discomfort—the recognition that lust and revenge should not be combined, that wild creatures and female figures should not be combined, that these combinations are taboo.

Hot button topics are taboo because they generate discomfort.

The male figure slakes his violent desires and is punished. The male figure also functions as a hot button, a means whereby the violent desires of tourists are slaked, while generating discomfort in these tourists.

The female figure slakes her sexual desires and is punished. The female figure also functions as a hot button, a means whereby the sexual desires of artists are slaked, while generating discomfort in these artists.

The tourist can climb into the rice chest. The tourist can pose for a photo in the rice chest. Then the tourist can climb out of the rice chest and walk away.

The artist can look into the hollow cow. The artist can render the contours of the hollow cow, the contours of the female figure. Then the artist can walk away.

Both containers allow the tourist and artist to touch the hot button, the taboo.

The desire and the discomfort remain contained.

Both containers allow the tourist and the artist to walk away.

The male and female figures remain contained.

Neither container—the rice chest, the hollow cow—appears to have any necessary connection to race.

To mention race where it is not necessary to mention race is taboo.

I have not mentioned the race of the tourist or the artist.

The tourist and the artist are allowed to pass for white.

The tourist and the artist are not contained.

I have already mentioned the race of the poet.

But to the extent that the poet is not contained, the poet is allowed to pass for white.

I have already mentioned the race of the male and female figures.

The male and female figures are contained.

The rice chest and the hollow cow are containers.

The rice chest and the hollow cow are not the only containers in this poem.

Colchis and Korea are containers in this poem.

Asianness is a container in this poem.

Race is a container in this poem.

Each of these containers contains desire and its satisfaction.

Each of these containers contains discomfort and deterrence.

Each of these containers contains a hot button, a taboo.

The tourist and the artist can enter each of these containers.

The tourist and the artist can touch the hot button and walk away.

Each of these containers separates the slaking of desire from the punishment of desire.

Each of these containers is an ingenious solution to a seemingly intractable problem.

They are the same problem.

They have the same solution.

Each of these containers ensures the frictionless transfer of power.

Each of these containers holds a male or female figure.

The name of the male figure can be translated as "Think of me in sadness."

The name of the female figure can be translated as "I shine for all of you."

from *Poetry*

My Life

◇ ◇ ◇

four years ago
on Martin Luther King Day
in the afternoon
the little strip
said it was time,
so we did it twice
laughing through
that grim comical
despair familiar
to all modern
conceivers,
it was magical
only that it worked
but now I know
it was then
my life began,
we made so
many plans
circumstances
already waited
to obviate,
suddenly he was born,
a room full of blood
and shouting,
he stayed calm
sleeping on my chest
a long time while
they sewed you up,
he and I

in a room alone
under a soft white light,
one nurse came
to say it was all right,
you were not
but you were there,
I talked to him,
whatever I said
I don't remember,
then came the proud
sleepless happy
sorrow months
then slow realizing
playground dread,
the year
of diagnosis when
our life kept
being a place
for worsening fears
in enviable comfort
to occur as we
graciously received
the humiliation
of being the ones
gratefully not to be,
those many hours
in the bedroom screaming
then lurching out
for exhausted walks,
trying with no
success to protect
us from everything
anyone could say,
gradually all our friends
and family lovingly
without intention
back into their lives
abandoned us,
we did not know
it was just us

growing stronger
in relation to a future
where no one
without permission
may join us,
now we're moving
fortunate ones
from our beloved house
to another on a hill
near a school
where his mind
happily alive
in music can grow,
can I say he is
my painful joy,
he thinks
in rhyme,
the truest friend
to no one yet
he is my
favorite word
remembrancer,
why am I telling you
you know it all
and yet to say
my version
of our story
in the morning
very early
imagining you
sitting behind me
touching my shoulder
scares and
comforts me,
before I go
I want to tell you
something new,
all the time
I walk around
thinking this life

yes but is this lovely
accident correct
and someday
how will it happen
to our bodies
and when it does
will we feel
like we lived
or just lived through

from *The New Yorker*

CONTRIBUTORS' NOTES AND COMMENTS

JULIA ALVAREZ writes poetry (*The Woman I Kept to Myself, The Other Side/El Otro Lado, Homecoming*), fiction (including *How the García Girls Lost Their Accents, In the Time of the Butterflies*, and the forthcoming *Afterlife*), essays, and books for young people of all ages. She divides her time unequally among these genres, but her first, beloved homeland is poetry, where—when the going gets tough, as in present-day USA—she finds herself returning for sanity, humanity, and hope.

Of "Saving the Children," Alvarez writes: "Like many others, I was riveted by the anguished, all-hands-on-deck/no-holds-barred rescue efforts to save the Wild Boars, a soccer team of twelve young boys (ages eleven to sixteen) and their coach trapped in a cave in Thailand flooding with torrential rainwater. The huge international coordination to save these children was happening at the same time (June/July 2018) that the first images came on the news of other children on our southern border (USA/Mexico) being separated from their parents in order to deter them from seeking asylum in this country. These disconnections—on the one hand, kindness and humanity; on the other, coldness and cruel indifference—are happening all the time, to be sure. But the irony of their proximity made it impossible to ignore. Our humanity can become trapped in our fears. The poem mounts its own rescue operation. We can become the good people we already are."

BRANDON AMICO was born in Boston, Massachusetts, in 1989. He is the author of a book of poems, *Disappearing, Inc.* (Gold Wake Press, 2019), and is the recipient of a fellowship from the National Endowment for the Arts and a grant from the North Carolina Arts Council.

Of "Customer Loyalty Program," Amico writes: "Humor has always been an oxygenating thing for me, and the more serious the topic (like our very survival in a societal machine that wants to break down, measure, and place value on each aspect of our selves), the more skepticism and irreverence is needed to create room to breathe. When concepts are puffed up to over-importance, you need to poke holes in them. John Cleese said that humor is right at home in serious discussions, but solemnity serves only *pomposity* and to guard the self-important from having their views questioned. I treat most 'givens' as suspect; any time we're told 'that's just the way it is/has always been,' a little flag should shoot up in the back of our minds, marking a point to be examined later.

"As such, despite its sardonic tone and above-quota number of sadomasochism references (I've read this poem at events in front of my parents before—it's awkward), I view 'Customer Loyalty Program' as an intensely serious poem that allowed me to tackle something significant—a generation coming of age in an economic climate that stripped so much of the physical and emotional security that those who came before us were more likely to enjoy. The absurdity invoked by the poem mirrors the absurdity present in many aspects of our lives today. Sometimes exaggerating feels the most honest."

RICK BAROT was born in the Philippines in 1969 and grew up in the San Francisco Bay Area. He is the author of four books of poems, most recently *The Galleons*, published in 2020 by Milkweed Editions. He lives in Tacoma, Washington, and directs the Rainier Writing Workshop, the low-residency MFA program at Pacific Lutheran University.

Barot writes: "The sequence excerpted here is from a ten-poem sequence titled 'The Galleons.' The sequence is about a lot of things, but at heart it's an elegy for my grandmother, who died in 2016 at ninety-two years old. One of the iconic images that I have of her life is when she traveled by ship from the Philippines to the United States in the late 1940s, with my grandfather and my toddler mother. It was a painful trip that took weeks across the Pacific. The image of her on that ship made me think of the long journey of her life, and how her migration story was haunted by the galleons' journeys across the same ocean centuries before, carrying their imperial and commercial cargo from the Philippines back to Spain. That juxtaposition—of vast differences of scale, of complicated intimacies between the past and the present—is what the sequence is ultimately about."

Born in Tehran, KAVEH BASSIRI is an Iranian American poet and translator. His chapbook *99 Names of Exile*, winner of the Anzaldúa Poetry Prize, was published in 2019 by Newfound. He received a 2019 translation fellowship from the National Endowment for the Arts.

Of "Invention of I," Bassiri writes, "It took me a long time to feel comfortable writing about my experience as an immigrant. If you migrate to another country when you are very young, you may forget your country of origin. If you come to another country when you are older, you will remain 'from' that country. But when you come to another country as a teenager, as I did, you always stay in-between, neither Iranian nor fully American. How can one see this condition not as a problem? It took years for me to accept a liminal life—and to appreciate this otherness that allowed me to see things in English and Persian I would not have been able to see otherwise.

"The poem deals with this in-between identity. It plays on grammatical rules of Persian and English. For example, the poem exploits the overuse of adjectives in Persian and the emphasis on nouns in English. But it goes beyond language and grammar. It reflects my personal experiences as well as explores what it means to be an Iranian or an American or both.

"The poem begins with 'In Farsi,' because it evokes the time I grew up in Iran and was learning English. (The Iranian language is called 'Farsi' in Iran.) The second part considers my life in America, where English is my main language and the Iranian language has become 'Persian.' Many of my friends insist that we should use the name 'Persian' for the Iranian language in English, just as we use 'German,' not 'Deutsch.' The debate over whether we should call my native tongue Persian or Farsi has been going on for a while, but I'm not making any specific point about that topic here. My use draws on a more personal experience of the role that these languages played in shaping who I am: a fractured 'I.'"

REGINALD DWAYNE BETTS is a poet, essayist, and memoirist. He was born in California in 1980. His most recent book, *Felon*, was published by W. W. Norton in 2019.

Of "A Man Drops a Coat on the Sidewalk and Almost Falls into the Arms of Another," Betts writes: "By way of statement: two decades ago, or nearly two decades ago, I began reading *The Best American Poetry*. Back then, sans MFA program, sans writing mentor, sans a functional library—the jewels I read in those editions pushed me. And my favorite part was the back of the book, the discourse that writers were having, I believed with me, about what sparked their poems. Because where does a poem come from?

"And, for me, this is straight narrative—first. If I'm lucky, it becomes other things. I want to say that the poem is what I saw, but that's never completely true. In that, even the photograph is selective sight; the poet, even more so. Still, I've begun to ask myself what does it mean to see what is close to you, and to see what is close to you in a way that obscures the stereotypes and clichés that drive so much of what passes for knowledge. This seeing is the essence of local noticing. Literally, me trying to capture this thing I saw, but do so in a way where it matters. And part of doing that was to cut out so much of what else I saw. The bit of trash on the ground, the weathered grass, the idle cars along the street. 'Cause don't knowing that junkies live and breathe and love and struggle out here matter? When I saw them, I wanted to see them. I remember the Richard Pryor bit about the wino and the junky. Pryor, brilliant at making you understand that he has noticed a thing that you didn't, and through characters, reveals how that noticing is what really matters. In that bit, you'll have to look it up, the junky says to the security guard: and who gonna clean up the blood? It's a perfect line—because it reveals that this cat has something to offer the world. I wanted to imagine that these men I watched in the thrall of a high, had something to offer the world even then.

"'Cause the casual story is that they are suffering, you believe they are blight. And shit, they were juxtaposed, in that moment, against the Winchester gun factory, what used to be one of the centers of the come up in New Haven—working-class work that ensured you could provide for a family. But that has long been closed. And the pair were also, visually, juxtaposed with a basketball court I've taken my sons to hoop at often. A court where my youngest once saw me win a game of 21 against two or three teenage boys—like late teens though, old enough to tire me out. And I'd won and leaped up as if I had won a chip, right. And so, I see the drug addicts, also young, and I want to tell the story in a way that doesn't belittle them.

"Own so fucking world. In the poem and in this life, I have no idea what that sentence means, but I know what it feels like. Like, reaching and holding something that matters and holding something that hurts and just dealing with it. I was with my friend Nicholas Dawidoff, which is to say, there was someone there reminding me of what matters in the world, and someone who could later check the vision of the poem. But I take it there is never a way to know that you got it right. Though, I do wish I could read the poem to the pair."

Born in Jamaica, Queens, in 1977, RYAN BLACK is the author of *The Tenant of Fire* (University of Pittsburgh Press), winner of the 2018

Agnes Lynch Starrett Poetry Prize, and *Death of a Nativist*, selected by Linda Gregerson for a Poetry Society of America chapbook fellowship. He is an assistant professor of English at Queens College of the City University of New York.

Black writes: " 'Nothing Beats a Fair' is part of a longer sequence of poems about Queens, New York, and what Joan Didion dismisses as 'the wastes of Queens.' Several relics of the 1964–65 World's Fair still stand in Flushing Meadows–Corona Park, evidence of a once imagined future for the city and the nation. Queens has long been seen as a harbinger of what the United States will one day become. More linguistically diverse. More ethnically and racially diverse. But 'Nothing Beats a Fair,' and the sequence it is part of, explore the complex, often contradictory, lived experience of this 'hyperdiversity,' to borrow a phrase from the ethnographer Ines Miyares, rather than the exoticizing or dismissal of its reality."

BRUCE BOND was born in Pasadena, California, in 1954. He is the author of twenty-five books including, most recently, *Blackout Starlight: New and Selected Poems, 1997–2015* (L.E. Phillabaum Award, LSU, 2017), *Rise and Fall of the Lesser Sun Gods* (Elixir Book Prize, Elixir Press, 2018), *Dear Reader* (Free Verse Editions, 2018), *Frankenstein's Children* (Lost Horse, 2018), *Plurality and the Poetics of Self* (Palgrave, 2019), and *Words Written Against the Walls of the City* (LSU, 2019). He is a Regents Professor of English at the University of North Texas.

Bond writes: "In 'Bells,' I wanted to explore the larger resonance— moral, political, and psychological—of the familiar koan: 'What is the sound of one hand clapping?' In one sense, it is the sound of bells, mourning the lost, christening a union, marking time. In another sense, it is all sound. Or rather, all that passes through us whose interpretive attention relies upon a dialogue between 'the two' and 'the one': difference and continuity, absence and presence, language and silence, pattern recognition and immediacies obscured by acts of power and transference gone awry. To name is both to connect and disconnect, to call and banish, to see and to risk mistaking our lenses for the seen. Misreading as such is both mother and child of our dread. In political terms, the problem of language and erasure correlates to that of democratic representation. How does one create a credible republic, which is to say, a social order where 'the one' articulates and honors the interests of the many? Words fail, but the aspiration is all. How might we better invoke 'the missing hand'? My hope here is to wed these questions to daily encounters with marginalization, to interrogate the minute unconscious mechanics of language, power, and all they might repress. Especially in an age where information is 'everywhere and nowhere,' which is to say, obscured via mass mediation, the integrity of the individual as both valued and seen has undergone a profound challenge. The problem is hardly new and hardly un-American, but the net amplifies our sense of cultural regression with unprecedented volume and velocity, such that it puts our childhood notions of America under pressure. Whatever that notion, it might serve us best as giving way to inner work and a style of attention less metaphysical and self-serving, less unfocused. Always something, someone, left out of the conversation, and so the summons to listen, act, see more clearly, unspeakably, to hear in the bells of every hour the silence of the mourned."

WILLIAM BREWER was born in West Virginia in 1989. He is the author of *I Know Your Kind* (Milkweed Editions, 2017), a winner of the National Poetry Series. Formerly a Stegner Fellow, he is now a Jones Lecturer at Stanford University.

Of "Orange," Brewer writes: "Paranoia is deranged creativity disguised under elegance. My hope was to capture its music and textures."

LUCIE BROCK-BROIDO (1956–2018) was the author of four books of poetry: *A Hunger*, *The Master Letters*, *Trouble in Mind*, and *Stay, Illusion*, which was a finalist for the 2013 National Book Award, the 2013 National Books Critics Circle Award, and the 2015 Kingsley Tufts Poetry Award. A recipient of the Harvard Phi Beta Kappa Teaching Award, the Harvard-Danforth Award for Distinction in Teaching, and Columbia University's Presidential Teaching Award, Brock-Broido was the director of poetry in the writing program at Columbia University School of the Arts from 1993 until her death on March 6, 2018.

When Ricardo Maldonado, interviewing Lucie for *Guernica* in 2013, asked her why she has devoted her life to teaching, she replied "I have made several vows in my life and I've never broken one yet. The first one, which I made when I was six, was that I would be a teacher. The second came right after that. All my hair was shorn off in a barber shop in Atlantic City. I swore, 'as god is my witness,' that no one would ever again cut my hair, not against my will. The third vow was that I would be a poet. The fourth was that my mother would never die. That was the only vow, to my knowledge, that I have ever broken. It wasn't that she would never die, but that she couldn't die, and then she did. I am a compulsive practitioner of magical thinking. And poetry is the skin that I have between my body and the world's body."

VICTORIA CHANG was born in Detroit, Michigan, in 1970. Her new book of poems, *Obit*, was published by Copper Canyon Press earlier this year. Other poetry books are *Barbie Chang*, *The Boss*, *Salvinia Molesta*, and *Circle*. Her children's picture book, *Is Mommy?*, was illustrated by Marla Frazee and published by Beach Lane Books/S&S. It was named a *New York Times* Notable Book. Her middle-grade novel, *Love, Love*, was published earlier this year by Sterling Publishing. She has received a Guggenheim Fellowship, the Poetry Society of America's Alice Fay Di Castagnola Award, and a Lannan Residency Fellowship. She lives in Los Angeles and is the program chair of Antioch's low-residency MFA program.

Chang writes: "A few of my *Obit* poems were published in last year's *Best American Poetry* and I wrote about their genesis there. In essence, my mother passed after a long illness and I was/am a bit lost without her. I read a lot of wonderful prose books during that time of intense grief, and while there were many poems that helped me, I can see, in retrospect, that I wrote these poems to help myself, to see if I could get to the center of grief. Could I distill it? Describe it? I'm not sure there is a center of grief now that I've written these poems. Grief is all around us all the time. It moves. It changes shape. I'm still grappling with grief now that my father, too, is nearing the end of his illness. But I'm trying to live with grief, not within it."

HEATHER CHRISTLE was born in Wolfeboro, New Hampshire, in 1980. She is the author of four poetry collections, most recently *Heliopause* (Wesleyan University Press, 2015). Her 2011 collection, *The Trees The Trees* (Octopus Books), won the Believer Poetry Award, served as the inspiration for the 2013 APRIL festival's art show, and was adapted into a ballet with music by Kyle Vegter and choreography by Robyn Mineko Williams. It premiered at the Pacific Northwest Ballet in 2019. *The Crying Book*, Christle's first work of nonfiction, was published by Catapult in the United States in November 2019. A German translation of the book came out simultaneously from Hanser, a UK edition from Corsair in February 2020, and many other translations are now underway. An audio adaptation of the book appeared on BBC Radio 4 in March. Christle recently joined the faculty of Emory University in Atlanta as assistant professor of English and creative writing.

Christle writes: "I have almost no recollection of writing this poem, perhaps because it happened more than ten years ago. All I know for sure is that the phrase 'The Waking Life' comes from a time when Lisa Olstein and I were generating titles to share across our poems, and this was one of her making. With more certainty I can say the poem's resurfacing came out of financial necessity. Last year, when I was without a steady job, and as my partner prepared to go on strike with his excellent faculty union, we faced the question of how to keep our family going without income for an unknown stretch of time. He came up with the idea of looking through my rather tall pile of unpublished poems, and sending some of them out to publications that pay poets for their work. For us, for our family, the ability of those journals and magazines to offer even token payments made a difference. We got through the strike—with the union victorious after three weeks of below freezing weather on the picket line—and this poem made its way into *Salamander*. I'm grateful to that publication, its workers, and all those who seek ways to help poets navigate the path of a life in the arts under capitalism."

AMA CODJOE was born in Austin, Texas, in 1979 and was raised in Youngstown, Ohio. She is the author of *Blood of the Air* (Northwestern University Press, 2020), winner of the Drinking Gourd Chapbook Poetry Prize. She has been awarded support from Cave Canem, the Jerome, Robert Rauschenberg, and Saltonstall foundations, as well as from Callaloo Creative Writing Workshop, Crosstown Arts, Hedgebrook, and the MacDowell Colony. She received a 2017 Rona Jaffe Writer's Award, *The Georgia Review*'s 2018 Loraine Williams Poetry Prize, a 2019 DISQUIET Literary Prize, a 2019 Oscar Williams and Gene Derwood Award, and a 2019 NEA Creative Writing Fellowship.

Deaf & genderqueer poet MEG DAY is the author of *Last Psalm at Sea Level* (Barrow Street, 2014), winner of the Publishing Triangle's Audre Lorde Award, and a finalist for the 2016 Kate Tufts Discovery Award. The 2015–2016 recipient of the Amy Lowell Poetry Traveling Scholarship and a 2013 recipient of an NEA Fellowship in Poetry, Day is the coeditor of *Laura Hershey: On the Life & Work of an American Master*, published in 2019 as a part of The Unsung Masters Series (Pleiades Press). Born in 1984 and raised in California, Day is currently assistant professor of English & Creative Writing at Franklin & Marshall College. www.megday.com

Of "In Line to Vote on Our Future Climate," Day writes: "When I wrote this poem, I was in a landlocked state & had just read an article about rising sea levels destroying—and disappearing—the Marshall Islands. The language in the report mirrored the casual & collective resignation that preceded the #MeToo movement & which we still employ in everyday sexism, a kind of boys-will-be-boys shrug toward the planet's collapse. It's easy for me to draw a line between what we are willing to do to each other & what we are willing to do to the planet. Given we are residents, aren't they often one & the same? In neither case is the doing passive, as much as we'd like to think it is, or relocate blame, shirk responsibility, or deny it altogether. I think our instinct is to turn toward the personal—to reject the real difficulty & labor of activism & instead dig down into the naïve safety of our beloveds, our kin. To shut out the world, or pretend we can, & claim it's all too little, too late. What does it mean to love another person through the swan song of the planet, to tend them in scarcity while refusing the earth? What does it mean to love women through the catastrophe we've made by enabling misogyny, & can we really call either disaster all that natural? I don't know if it's possible to write a love poem right now that isn't deeply politicized. Every action or inaction is a vote we make with our lives."

TIMOTHY DONNELLY was born in Providence, Rhode Island, in 1969. His most recent publications include *The Problem of the Many* (Wave Books, 2019) and *The Cloud Corporation* (Wave Books, 2010), winner of the 2012 Kingsley Tufts Poetry Award. A Guggenheim Fellow, he is currently director of poetry in the writing program of Columbia University's School of the Arts. He lives in Brooklyn with his family.

Donnelly writes: "I wrote 'All Through the War' toward the middle of 2018, a year that seemed to go out of its way to make me want to hate it. Many of the challenges it set for my family and for me are alluded to throughout the poem, as are the nations our nation was in combat with, or in, at the time. The point isn't, of course, to compare personal suffering with suffering that takes place on a much greater scale and with far more complex implications, but rather to reflect on how both kinds of suffering will happen simultaneously, with the former sometimes distracting our attention from the latter in a way that is no less problematic for being kind of inevitable. The poem tries to widen its circumference in order to accommodate as much knowledge as it can, even to the point of documenting items of no apparent consequence, but it does so in the hope of keeping everything it remembers, even the merest debris of a life, from folding into oblivion. I have come to think of this as one of the two most important tasks a poem can set out to do."

Born in Houston in 1996, HAZEM FAHMY is a poet and critic from Cairo. He is currently pursuing his MA in Middle Eastern studies and film studies at the University of Texas at Austin. His debut chapbook, *Red//Jild//Prayer*, won the 2017 Diode Editions Contest. His performances have been featured on Button Poetry and Write About Now. A Kundiman and Watering Hole Fellow, he is a reader for the *Shade Journal*, and a contributing writer to *Film Inquiry*.

VIEVEE FRANCIS is the author of three books of poetry: *Blue-Tail Fly* (Wayne State University Press, 2006), *Horse in the Dark* (winner of the Cave Canem Northwestern University Poetry Prize for a second collection; Northwestern University Press, 2016), and *Forest Primeval* (winner of the Hurston Wright Legacy Award and the 2017 Kingsley Tufts Poetry Award; Triquarterly, 2015). Her work has appeared in the *The Best American Poetry* (2010, 2014, 2017, and 2019 editions), and *Angles of Ascent: A Norton Anthology of Contemporary African American Poetry*. She has been a poet-in-residence for the Alice Lloyd Scholars Program at the University of Michigan and teaches poetry writing in the Callaloo Creative Writing Workshop (United States, UK, and Barbados). In 2009 she received a Rona Jaffe Writer's Award, and in 2010, a Kresge Fellowship. An associate editor of *Callaloo*, she is an associate professor of English and creative writing at Dartmouth College in Hanover, New Hampshire.

RACHEL GALVIN's books of poetry include *Elevated Threat Level*, which was a finalist for the National Poetry Series, and *Pulleys & Locomotion*. Her translations include Raymond Queneau's *Hitting the Streets*, which won the Scott Moncrieff Prize for translation, and *Decals: Complete Early Poetry of Oliverio Girondo*, a finalist for the National Translation Award (cotranslated with Harris Feinsod). Her translation of *Cowboy & Other Poems*, a chapbook by Alejandro Albarrán Polanco, was just published by Ugly Duckling Presse. Galvin is a cofounder of Outranspo, an international creative translation collective (www.outranspo.com). She was born in Boston in 1975 and now lives in Chicago, where she is associate professor of English and comparative literature at the University of Chicago and associate director of the creative writing program.

Galvin writes: "I wrote 'Little Death' after watching a short film by the remarkable Brazilian artist Jonathas de Andrade called *O Peixe (The Fish)*."

JULIAN GEWIRTZ, born in 1989 in New Haven, Connecticut, is a historian and poet. He is currently a postdoctoral scholar at Harvard University and is the author of a history of China's economic transformation, *Unlikely Partners* (Harvard University Press, 2017), and a new history of the tumult and legacies of the 1980s (forthcoming from Harvard). He writes regularly for publications such as *The Guardian*, the *New York Times*, and the *Wall Street Journal*.

Gewirtz writes: " 'To X (Written on This Device You Made)' is part of a larger book manuscript, *Your Face, My Flag*, which investigates the place of the lyric speaker in a globalized era that is alienated from its history and shaped by escalating tensions between China and 'the West.' This poem responds to the extraordinary collection *Iron Moon: An Anthology of Chinese Worker Poetry*, edited by Qin Xiaoyu and translated by Eleanor Goodman. It also adapts language from Chinese and English media reports on the suicides at the Foxconn facilities in mainland China where iPhones are assembled. The experience of Chinese workers—and the intimate connection to their exploitation of every person who wears 'Made in China' clothing or texts on an iPhone—is almost wholly absent from mainstream conversations in the United States, even though those workers' labor has reshaped our world. I hope that this poem can, in a small way, contribute to remedying that imbalance."

Born in Brooklyn in 1967, REGAN GOOD attended Barnard College and the Iowa Writers' Workshop. She published her first book, *The Atlantic House*, in 2011 and *The Needle* in 2020. She teaches poetry and writing at Barnard College and the Pratt Institute.

Of "Birches Are the Gods' Favorite Tree," Good writes: "I had been talking to a friend, a painter and poet, about birch trees and their immense root systems. We decided that [a] god or the gods would favor drawings over paintings, drawings being the understructure of things—like the birches' roots. A few days later on Facebook (that heinous scourge), a clip of a live skinned dog popped up on my feed. I have no idea what happened to the dog, I could barely look at the video for more than a second, but I saw everything. I wish I could forget, though even if I could, I know that worse suffering happens, and has happened. The world throws up unspeakable horror and pain into our lives. The randomness of suffering and grief is at the heart of the poem. No laws decide who suffers here. What kind of God lets their creatures suffer like this dog? How are we supposed to carry on, as Berryman wrote, to 'bear & be,' in a world where a dog can be skinned alive and walk out of the abattoir seeking comfort? The salts of the world can be excruciating. Somewhere always, every second of the day a slaughterhouse is at work. Every day is a 'cathedral tune' somewhere, for someone, for some bewildered creature, human or animal, who did nothing wrong. It is not really bearable, but we bear it."

CHRISTINE GOSNAY was born in Baltimore, Maryland, in 1981. Her first book, *Even Years* (Kent State University Press, 2017), won the Stan and Tom Wick Poetry Prize. Her chapbook, *The Wanderer*, is the 2019 title in *Beloit Poetry Journal*'s Chad Walsh Chapbook series. She lives in California.

Gosnay writes: "This is a poem that I composed, in my small blue bedroom, in the course of a single April afternoon, more or less in a single hour. I normally revise poems by closing my eyes and rewriting them from memory; whatever remains tends to be the finished poem (an actual 're-vision' of the work). The day after I wrote 'Sex,' I read it and decided not to do anything of the sort, and sent it off into the world the way it was without wondering much about what would happen to it or who might read it. I considered it a complete unit of expression and feeling that I was finished with. When I read it now, I find it not at all surprising, neither good nor bad, neither finished nor unfinished; rather, it seems a strange location in my memory, an unabashed representation of my thoughts on that April afternoon."

JORIE GRAHAM is the author of fourteen collections of poetry, including, recently, *Fast* and *Runaway,* both from Ecco/HarperCollins. She has published two volumes of selected poetry, *The Dream of the Unified Field*, which was awarded the Pulitzer Prize in 1996, and *From the New World*. Graham was born in New York City in 1950, was raised in Italy, and only returned to the United States to finish her education. She currently lives in Massachusetts and teaches at Harvard University.

Of "It Cannot Be," Graham writes: "On the surface, this poem was prompted by memories of visits to the southern Italian coastline, where hundreds of people have perished in their attempt to cross the Mediterranean and escape civil war, drought, and other atrocities inflicted upon them in the northern regions of Africa—though many have traveled from far within the Continent to reach the shore. I say 'memories' because those nightmares were reawakened for me by the humanitarian crisis on our southern border, especially the forced separation of infants & children from their mothers and fathers."

SAMUEL GREEN was born in Sedro-Woolley, Washington, in 1948. For nearly forty years he has lived off the grid on a small Pacific Northwest island where he has been coeditor of the Brooding Heron Press with his wife, Sally. His collections of poetry include *The Grace of Necessity* (2008), *All That Might Be Done* (2014), and *Disturbing the Light* (2020), all from Carnegie Mellon University Press. A visiting professor at multiple colleges and universities, he was selected as the first poet laureate of Washington State. In 2018, he was awarded an honorary doctorate from Seattle University. From 1966 to 1970, he was in the U.S. Coast Guard, with service in Vietnam.

Of "On Patmos, Kneeling in the Panagia," Green writes: "After the accident mentioned in the poem—which occurred in September 1969—I was in a leg cast for more than two years, so the circumstances of the injury were much on my mind. Early drafts date from 1971, when I was taking notes for a writing class, but I couldn't make the poem work. Over the years I told the story to friends and tried to find some way to discover poetry in it, but kept failing. Then, a few years ago, symptoms of late onset PTSD began developing, and I began getting vivid flashbacks. Poems about events I'd been suppressing for fifty years began developing, but I found myself avoiding the hospital encounter I had witnessed. Then, after finishing a poem about witnessing a soldier's death in Vung Tau, I revisited notes I'd made and remembered how, at a Mass on the island of Patmos, the sound of high heels on cobblestones had brought back the sound of a woman's shoes in the hospital, and the piece resolved itself in a matter of days in fewer than fifty drafts. I had to grow up enough to realize the poem was about her and not me."

Born in Fall River, Massachusetts, in the great year of 1984 (not just a book!), BC GRIFFITH lives around Brooklyn where he tends to his favorite house plants and watches reruns on TV. More about his work can be found at Betacrow.com.

Of "Big Gay Ass Poem," Griffith writes: "Thanks to those who enjoyed grappling with this poem, or to those who got a laugh out of it.

Having this poem appear in such a venerable publication has given me an unusual occasion to puzzle over my own work as well as a profound sense of Imposter Syndrome. This poem was written in the spring of 2017: a dynamic time for the United States, and a terrifying time for the LGBTQIA community. It harbors my usual homosexual anxieties about the world: how gay bodies should look, should act, should feel, especially in unfamiliar or unsafe spaces; how gay bodies should perform to avoid 'detection'; and the humor caught in a 'false positive' (being called gay as an insult, not an identification). Gays in space—in all their intersectional glory—remains a topic to confound my work, and I hope it continues to help me produce poems at a fecund depth. Thanks, too, to my ass, for being the right piece at the wrong time, and for everyone who carries these intimate burdens with them."

RACHEL ELIZA GRIFFITHS was born in Washington, D.C., in 1978. Her most recent book is *Seeing the Body* (W. W. Norton, 2020).

Of "Good Mother," Griffiths writes: "In one of my most ugliest moments of grief after my mother's death, I was saved by a stranger's kindness and will. This unnamed woman, wherever she is, exists as a presence I can still sometimes feel holding me. I hope this poem finds its way to her in the terrifying way her kindness found me in the middle of an ordinary day and reminded me that I once believed in miracles. Maybe I still do."

JENNIFER GROTZ was born in Canyon, Texas, in 1971. She is a professor at the University of Rochester as well as director of the Bread Loaf Writers' Conferences. She is the author of three books of poetry, most recently *Window Left Open* (Graywolf Press, 2016). She has translated, from the French, the novel *Rochester Knockings* by Hubert Haddad (Open Letter, 2015) and *Psalms of All My Days*, poems by Patrice de La Tour du Pin (Carnegie Mellon University Press, 2013). *Everything I Don't Know*, the selected poems of Jerzy Ficowski, cotranslated from the Polish with Piotr Sommer, is forthcoming in late 2020 by World Poetry Books. This is her fifth appearance in *The Best American Poetry* series.

Grotz writes: "'The Conversion of Paul' is addressed to my late dear friend Paul Otremba. In the drafting of it, I allowed myself to speak honestly in a kind of unrelenting outpour, seeking to make sense of, to say something true about, the startling coincidence of finding out about Paul's cancer diagnosis while I was in Italy and where, in fact, I'd visited a painting we both loved and about which he'd written an extraordinary poem ('Surfing for Caravaggio's "Conversion of Paul"'). For the reader, then, the poem is a kind of eavesdropping in on a conversation, but for the poet, it's also a meditation on poetry-as-conversation in the first place, how it is overheard, considered, and repeated over time. My poem is in conversation with Paul and his poem is in conversation with his late teacher Stanley Plumly's poem, which is conversing with Thom Gunn's poem about this same Caravaggio painting in Santa Maria del Popolo.

"'Eloquence is heard, poetry is overheard,' John Stuart Mill once observed. What I hope the reader gleans from such overhearing is my gratitude for the conversations that poems and paintings and other works of art continue to provide me, but most importantly for the admiration and love I have for my friend."

CAMILLE GUTHRIE's new book, *Diamonds*, is forthcoming from BOA Editions in fall 2021. She is the author of three books of poetry: *Articulated Lair: Poems for Louise Bourgeois* (2013), *In Captivity* (2006), and *The Master Thief* (2000), all published by Subpress. Her poems have appeared in *The Best American Poetry 2019* and *Art & Artists: Poems* (Everyman's Library). Born in Seattle in 1971, she has lived in Pittsburgh and Brooklyn; currently, she lives in rural Vermont with her two children. She holds an MFA from Brown University and a BA from Vassar College and has been awarded fellowships from the MacDowell Colony and the Yaddo Foundation. She is the director of the undergraduate writing initiatives at Bennington College.

Of "During the Middle Ages," Guthrie writes: "Sei Shōnagon (c. 966–c. 1025) wrote in 'Hateful Things' from *The Pillow Book* (*Makura no Sōshi*): 'A man who has nothing in particular to recommend him discusses all sorts of subjects at random as though he knew everything' (translated by Ivan Morris in 1967). Before my midforties, I thought that a midlife crisis was a joke—a phase that men went through, then bought themselves red cars. I was wrong, and life's mean joke was on me. During that hard time, I searched for strategies to cope with my sadness; self-help books did little for me, yet I discovered that I already had a strangely comforting habit of mind: when we would lose power in a snowstorm, for example, I would think, 'I'm a frontier woman!' The electricity would come back on in hours, and I was not, of course, someone crossing the mountains and stealing people's land. At that time, I also heard mean internal voices telling me that I was unlovable;

I had lost my confidence, sense of humor, and feminism. Once the pun occurred to me, I wrote down everything awful I could remember from Medieval Times (buboes!) and quickly slipped into that familiar fantasy of imagining oneself as someone heroic in a previous life. How wonderful it would be to be, or to know, Sei Shōnagon! It became a pleasurable habit to think of girlfriends from history who also struggled with despair and the patriarchy; it helped me to appreciate the present and the girlfriends who rescued me with their humor and confidence. It's hard enough to be a woman now, but I can vote. And I will."

JANICE N. HARRINGTON was born in Vernon, Alabama, in 1956. Her collections include *Primitive: The Art and Life of Horace H. Pippin* (BOA Editions, 2016), *The Hands of Strangers* (BOA Editions, 2011) and *Even the Hollow My Body Made Is Gone* (BOA Editions, 2007). She also writes children's books. Harrington teaches creative writing at the University of Illinois.

Harrington writes: "Memory of a shattered family heirloom triggered 'Putting the Pieces Together.' Anna slowly glued the broken pieces together. Lesson #1: Never waste beauty. Lesson #2: It is not the breaks that matter. I wanted to enact a sense of physically bringing the parts of the poem together (aggressive enjambments, disjunctive leaps, and uncomfortable line breaks) and the difficulty of sealing memory, social history, lived experience, and the frictions of race together with the frailest glue of all: words."

TONY HOAGLAND (1953–2018) published seven books of poetry, including *Priest Turned Therapist Treats Fear of God* (2018), *What Narcissism Means to Me* (2003) and, winner of the James Laughlin Award, *Donkey Gospel* (1998), each from Graywolf Press. His third collection of essays, *The Underground Poetry Metro Transportation System for Souls: Essays on the Cultural Life of Poetry*, was published in 2019 (University of Michigan Press). Also published in 2019: a craft book, with Kay Cosgrove, *The Art of Voice: Poetic Principles and Practices* (W. W. Norton). *Cinderbiter: Celtic Poems*, with Martin Shaw, was published by Graywolf in 2020.

Tony Hoagland wrote with great humor and daring. In the context of various isms (including Communism, Capitalism, Feminism, and Catholicism) he praised narcissism as "the system that means the most to me." He could sound a defiant note. In a poem in *What Narcissism*

Means to Me, he writes that some people think he should end up in a room alone with a gun and "a bottle of hate." But the hatred makes him strong, he says, "and my survival is their failure." The poet concludes that he loves his "November life, / where I run like a train / deeper and deeper / into the land of my enemies."

KIMBERLY JOHNSON was born in Salt Lake City, Utah, in 1971. She is the author of three collections of poetry, most recently *Uncommon Prayer* (Persea, 2014), and of book-length translations of Latin and Greek poetry. Her scholarly work on sixteenth- and seventeenth-century literature appears widely. With Jay Hopler, she edited *Before the Door of God: An Anthology of Devotional Poetry* (Yale University Press, 2013). She is the recipient of fellowships and awards from the Guggenheim Foundation and the NEA.

Johnson writes: "'Fifteen' began its life as a slant of sunlight through the glass ceiling of the Old Masters Museum in Brussels, which fell upon two Brueghel paintings: *Landscape with the Fall of Icarus* and *The Fall of the Rebel Angels*. I was thinking, perhaps inescapably, of Auden's great poem on the former, but my two teenaged children seemed indifferent to its pastoral scene beside the pandemonium of the latter. I watched my boys, each edging further into adolescence and its necessary separations, framed in shafts of sun and pointing out one surprise after another, as if the painting were a seek-and-find game from which I was excluded. The photograph I snapped at that moment is among my favorite pictures."

TROY JOLLIMORE was born in Liverpool, Nova Scotia, in 1971. He is the author of three books of poems: *Tom Thomson in Purgatory* (2006), *At Lake Scugog* (2011), and *Syllabus of Errors* (2015). *Tom Thomson in Purgatory* won the National Book Critics Circle Award. As a philosopher he has written *On Loyalty* and *Love's Vision*. He has received fellowships from the Stanford Humanities Center, the Bread Loaf Writers' Conference, and the Guggenheim Foundation.

Of "The Garden of Earthly Delights," Jollimore writes: "This poem came in stages, and the first lines were the last to be written. I knew from the start that I wanted to end with the idea of a return to earth, with an affirmation of earthbound love, and of course with a reference to *Solaris*. I wanted the poem to move from one kind of visual art to another, in part as a way of evoking changes in human culture over the past few hundred years, connected, perhaps, to changes that have affected how people might tend to think about the planet, the value of the natural world, and the very idea of 'home.'

"So the ending was fairly apparent. What was less apparent, in the early stages, was the beginning, our way into the poem. I had been thinking and writing about similarities and differences between poetry and other art forms, and in particular about the kinds of ambiguities that are possible in painting, because of the way that we viewers tend to interact with the still scenes depicted in paintings, by projecting various narratives and interpretations onto them. Moreover, questions of projection and interpretation are also at the heart both of Tarkovsky's *Solaris* and of the Stanislaw Lem novel on which the film is based. And I was intrigued by the way Bosch's painting, both because, like any painting, it depicts still moments frozen in time, but also because it is divided into three parts with undefined relationships between them, leaves it open just how the various actions and consequences are related to one another, and how orderly this vision of the cosmos is intended to be.

"This openness—this mystery—is, I think, part of the core of any successful work of art. And once it became clear that this was a central concern of the poem, the first few lines came fairly easily; all that was left was to rearrange the remainder, and drop a couple passages that now seemed extraneous. One could contest pretty much every claim the poem makes. But whatever the job of a poet might be—and I am still trying to work that out to my own satisfaction—I'm fairly certain that it isn't to advance safe, uncontroversial claims that are immune to doubt or challenge."

ILYA KAMINSKY was born in Odessa, in the former Soviet Union, in 1977. He is the author of *Dancing in Odessa* (Tupelo Press, 2004) and *Deaf Republic* (Graywolf Press, 2019), where the poem included here appears. He is the coeditor of *The Ecco Anthology of International Poetry* (HarperCollins) and cotranslator of *Dark Elderberry Branch: Poems of Marina Tsvetaeva* (Alice James, 2012). He lives in Atlanta.

Of "In a Time of Peace," Kaminsky writes: "I wrote this poem after seeing Carolyn Forché interview Patricia Smith on stage, right after Trump's election. The poem is dedicated to Carolyn and Patricia."

Born in Brooklyn in 1974, DOUGLAS KEARNEY was raised in Altadena, California. He is a Foundation for Contemporary Arts Cy Twombly awardee and Cave Canem fellow. His six books include *Buck Studies* and *The Black Automaton*. He teaches creative writing at the University of Minnesota–Twin Cities. He lives in St. Paul, Minnesota, with his family.

Of "Sho," Kearney writes: "I teach a course in which students develop new poetic forms. Indigo Weller, now an alum of CalArts' Creative Writing MFA (where I used to teach), created the torchon, which has some similarities to the sestina, but derives its patterns of interweaving teleutons from lacemaking. The torchon has other formal and content constraints as well as structural conventions, including a consistent syllabic measure across the tercets, a scene of difficulty in which the speaker is also implicated/oriented, and a sense of return."

DONIKA KELLY was born in Los Angeles, California, in 1983. She is the author of *The Renunciations* (forthcoming), *Bestiary* (Graywolf Press, 2016), and the chapbook *Aviarium*.

Of "I Never Figured How to Get Free," Kelly writes: "This poem tries to capture the feeling of being complicit in ongoing U.S. military action, particularly in the Middle East, which has been the backdrop of most of my life. I wanted to write about how it felt to be a citizen of an imperialist nation seemingly always at war when the war is distant and on a screen."

CHRISTOPHER KEMPF was born in Marion, Ohio, in 1985. He is the author of the poetry collections *Late in the Empire of Men* and *What Though the Field Be Lost* (forthcoming from Louisiana State University Press in 2021). He has received a National Endowment for the Arts Fellowship and a Wallace Stegner Fellowship from Stanford University. He holds a PhD in English literature from the University of Chicago.

Kempf writes: "My poem 'After,' originated during the year I spent as an emerging writer/lecturer at Gettysburg College, where I was struck nearly every day by how immediate American history can feel. The poem endeavors to think through the multiple and conflicting ways in which the Civil War is commemorated, drawing in particular on Christian mythology to figure the war as a form of rebirth or national 'starting-over.' In some ways, it was; in many others, it was not. At the same time, the poem argues for the kind of capacious ethics so prominent in the aftermath of the Civil War, a time, for example, when former Confederate general James Longstreet led black freedom fighters against Southern militias composed of his own former soldiers."

STEVEN KLEINMAN is the winner of the 2019 Philip Levine Poetry Prize, and his first book, *Life Cycle of a Bear*, will be published by Anhinga Press in 2021. He is a contributing editor at *The American Poetry Review*, where he helps to host the *American Poetry Review Podcast*. He is the coordinator of the Art Alliance Writers' Workshop at the University of the Arts where he teaches poetry. He earned his MFA from the University of Maryland.

Kleinman writes: "I hesitate to unpack or decode the poem. I will say that it is the second poem in a sequence of four poems also titled 'Bear.' The poems deal with the figure of Bear, using him in many ways—often unkindly. This particular draft was written during a time that I was deeply worried about the future of Bear. Perhaps I still am. Perhaps I'm even more worried now than I was at the time I wrote the poem. I love how the form, a long rambling sequence of questions, allows for so much exploration."

JENNIFER L. KNOX's fifth book of poems, *Crushing It*, will be published by Copper Canyon Press in Fall 2020. She holds an MFA from New York University and has received an Iowa Arts Council Fellowship. She teaches at Iowa State University and is the proprietor of Saltlickers, a small-batch artisanal spice company. This is her fifth appearance in the *Best American Poetry* series.

Of "The Gift," Knox writes: "I'm always holding a handful of ideas for poems in my head. When I try to write about *one* of them, the end result's often a little flat, I think, because I'd already decided on the subject before I sat down to write. Where's the discovery in that? But if I bring *two* ideas together—especially unrelated ones—the ideas have to learn how to talk to each other. That's the discovery.

"A few years after my mother generously bought me a car, I mentioned it to my friend, Ada, who was surprised, because I hadn't told her, which suggested to me that I was hiding it from her and myself. I was, in some way, ashamed that I needed my mother, and that she could help me. I knew instantly that this occasion called for a poem, but how to get into it?

"Ten years ago, I worked with a hilarious guy named Steve and was accompanied by Gobi, a caged Quaker parrot that belonged to our eccentric boss. I knew nothing about birds, but I kept Gobi in my office, talked to him, shared my lunch with him, and let him chew on my shoelaces while I studied birds on the internet. The beginning of the poem is one of the first facts I learned about captive birds: if it looks like it's wearing a pipe cleaner wig, like Gobi did, it's mateless (eventually, I did learn to attend to Gobi's pinfeathers). I told Steve (who happened to be single) my discovery. The next day, he burst into my office and said, 'I dreamt that someone removed all my pin feathers!'

" 'Does that mean you're signing up for Match.com?' I asked, but he didn't see the connection.

"So the poem starts in one of my favorite stories about showing love, and ends in another story about showing love that I didn't know I knew until I wrote the poem."

YUSEF KOMUNYAKAA was born in Bogalusa, Louisiana, in 1947. His forthcoming volume of new and selected poems, *Everyday Mojo Songs of Earth*, will be available from Farrar, Straus and Giroux in 2020. He was the guest editor of *The Best American Poetry 2003*. He teaches at New York University.

Of "The Jungle," Komunyakaa writes: "I feel that Wifredo Lam's surrealism has chosen me. I was introduced to the painter's work through Aimé Césaire's poetry more than three decades ago. And from the onset, I could feel how the vision of the poet from Martinique and the painter from Cuba converge at times—as if through an unspoken dialogue connected by subject matter and feeling. Matter-of-fact, a study for 'The Jungle' that is at the Art Institute in Chicago appears on the cover of my book *Pleasure Dome* (2001). Though we never met, I daresay that I know this artist, this man, this dreamer who possessed a mysterious third eye.

"My in-progress series *Wishbone Trilogy* (the first book of which, *Taboo*, appeared in 2004) is devoted to exacting tribute poems—all in tercets—mainly dedicated to black and indigenous musicians and artists. This poem, 'The Jungle,' commissioned by MoMA, also belongs in the trilogy. I tend to ingest feelings, thoughts, and knowledge, and then, through form and sound, shift toward improvisation and imagination.

"The ending of the poem rises out of insinuation; no, 'I put a spell on you' isn't Screamin' Jay Hawkins, but I hear and feel vintage Nina Simone—still on the night streets of literary Paris—bringing it all back to Africa."

NICK LANTZ was born in Berkeley, California, in 1980. He is currently an associate professor at Sam Houston State University, where he teaches in the MFA in creative writing, editing, and publishing and is the editor of the *Texas Review*. He is the author of four collections of poetry: *We Don't Know We Don't Know* (Graywolf Press, 2010), *The Lightning That Strikes the Neighbors' House* (University of Wisconsin Press, 2010), *How to Dance as the Roof Caves In* (Graywolf Press, 2014), and *You, Beast* (University of Wisconsin Press, 2017).

Of "After a Transcript of the Final Voicemails of 9/11 Victims," Lantz writes: "This poem began with my attempt to write directly about—and include—transcriptions of actual 9/11 victim voicemails, but very quickly I decided that this method felt cheap and flat, so I tried to be more associational, to approach the topic asymptotically. As with most of the poems I was working on at the time, I wanted to allow contradictory ideas to interweave and coexist within the poem. In this case, I was thinking about ephemerality and endurance, how phenomena that are inherently fleeting can still persist in ways that feel indelible, and how easy it can be to forget the unforgettable. The poem uses a variety of sound-related anecdotes to explore those contradictions, though it doesn't try to resolve them. Instead, the poem ends with an image of recognition, an idea I've been preoccupied with lately. For a long time, I assumed that a political poem was primarily an act of persuasion, which is something I've never believed poems are especially good at. But for the last few years, I've been thinking of such poems less as persuasion and more as acknowledgment, as a way of expressing solidarity, of affirming and recognizing our experiences in a world that often seeks to ignore or deny them."

SHARA LESSLEY was born in Visalia, California, in 1975. She is the author of *The Explosive Expert's Wife*, *Two-Headed Nightingale*, and coeditor of *The Poem's Country: Place & Poetic Practice*. A former Wallace Stegner Fellow in Poetry, she has won a National Endowment for the Arts Fellowship, the Mary Wood Fellowship from Washington College, the Diane Middlebrook Poetry Fellowship from the Wisconsin Institute for Creative Writing, and an Olive B. O'Connor Fellowship from Colgate University. She is assistant poetry editor for Acre Books and lives in Dubai.

Lessley writes: "The first line of 'On Faith' came to me in 2005 on a snowy walk in central New York. I tried for years to build a poem around those ten syllables, but always fell short. Still, the words haunted me. I never forgot them. May 2018: a year and a half after his youngest sister took her life, one of my closest childhood friends committed suicide in his backyard. Both siblings were Evangelical Christians. A lapsed Catholic, I have long struggled with clinical depression, as well as with matters of doubt and belief. After my return to England (where I lived at the time) from the funeral in California, a draft of the poem came quickly. Initially, I made the mistake of calling it 'On Grief.' And while loss is certainly central to 'On Faith,' it is acceptance and conviction—particularly, in the face of recurring despair—that truly anchors the poem. In fact, typing this, I now see that holding on for thirteen years to that refrain (*there is no map for how the apples fall*)—never knowing what, if anything would become of it, never anticipating how completely it would serve as a source of comfort during a period of great confusion and mourning—isn't that, too, a steadfastness not entirely unlike what some believers experience as faith?"

STEVEN LEYVA was born in New Orleans, Louisiana, in 1982 and was raised in Houston, Texas. His first full-length collection, *The Understudy's Handbook*, received the Jean Feldman Book Award from Washington Writers Publishing House and is forthcoming in 2020. He is a Cave Canem fellow and author of the chapbook *Low Parish*. He holds an MFA from the University of Baltimore, where he is an assistant professor in the Klein Family School of Communications Design.

Of "When I Feel a Whoop Comin' On," Leyva writes: "Perhaps we spend our whole lives learning and unlearning the poetics of middle school dances."

CATE LYCURGUS was born in California in 1988 and received her MFA from Indiana University. The recipient of fellowships from the Bread Loaf and Sewanee Writers' Conferences, she was named one of *Narrative*'s Under 30 Featured Writers. She lives south of San Francisco where she interviews for *32 Poems* and teaches professional writing.

Of "Locomotion," Lycurgus writes: "As a daily runner, caretaker, and all-around active person, I grew fairly surly one spring with a spine injury that wouldn't go away. My complaints seemed all the more ridiculous in light of my quadriplegic father who had not stood in decades; or my grandfather, who worked on the railroad and, like so many, depended on his body for a living. Still, regardless of one's physicality, it is never easy to reconcile a body that will not oblige. And so I began to poem this out—the first lines haunted as I tried to run and the rest only clicked weeks later, once my spine moved into place. Reminding me just how much I'm at the mercy of body and breath, and how the real challenge is for the spirit to align—to let it."

KHALED MATTAWA was born in Benghazi, Libya, in 1964. He has pub-lished five books of poems, most recently *Mare Nostrum* (Sarabande, 2019). He translates poetry and has edited anthologies of Arab Amer-ican writing. Recipient of a MacArthur Foundation Fellowship, he teaches at the University of Michigan and edits the *Michigan Quarterly Review*.

JENNIFER MILITELLO was born in New York, New York, in 1975. She is the author of four collections of poetry, including, most recently, *A Camouflage of Specimens and Garments* (Tupelo Press, 2016) and *Body Thesaurus* (Tupelo Press, 2013), as well as the memoir *Knock Wood*, winner of the 2018 Dzanc Nonfiction Prize. She teaches in the MFA program at New England College.

Of "The Punishment of One Is the Love Song of Another," Militello writes: "I wrote this poem at Penn Station while waiting to catch a train. It is one of a series of poems exploring romantic love as a source of affliction as well as bliss. We are taught by movies and televi-sion that love will cure the sense of isolation in us, the feeling that we are alone and misunderstood. And what is complex about the best love affairs is often what makes them worthwhile. But if we are fortunate enough to find someone who can recognize us fully, and to give our-selves up to that love, the ardor itself can become a source of harm. My series of poems is in conversation with *The World Before Snow* by Brit-ish poet Tim Liardet."

SUSAN LESLIE MOORE was born in San Diego, California, in 1963. She is the author of *That Place Where You Opened Your Hands* (University of Massachusetts Press), winner of the Juniper Prize in poetry in 2019. She is the director of programs for writers at Literary Arts in Portland, Oregon.

Moore writes: "I wrote 'Night of the Living' not long after I discov-ered a stargazer app that identifies the constellations when you point your phone at the sky. I was intrigued by the sheer volume of stars and the way we live under constellations that were named so long ago, their relationship to the present, and how naming things gives them energy and power."

JOHN MURILLO is the author of the poetry collections *Up Jump the Boo-gie* (Cypher, 2010; Four Way Books, 2020), finalist for both the Kate Tufts Discovery Award and the PEN Open Book Award, and *Kontem-*

porary Amerikan Poetry (Four Way, 2020). He has received fellowships from the National Endowment for the Arts, the Bread Loaf Writers' Conference, Fine Arts Work Center in Provincetown, Cave Canem Foundation, and the Wisconsin Institute for Creative Writing. His work has appeared in two previous editions of *The Best American Poetry*. He is an assistant professor of English at Wesleyan University and teaches in the low-residency MFA program at Sierra Nevada College. He lives in Brooklyn.

Of "A Refusal to Mourn the Deaths, by Gunfire, of Three Men in Brooklyn," Murillo writes: "The title is a nod to Dylan Thomas's famous poem, 'A Refusal to Mourn the Death, by Fire, of a Child in London.' The poem itself was written in part as a reflection on police-community relations since the 1992 uprisings, and partly as a response to the killing of two NYPD officers and subsequent suicide of twenty-eight-year-old Ishmael Brinsley. On December 20, 2014, Brinsley shot and killed Brooklyn officers Rafael Ramos and Wenjian Liu, before fleeing the scene and ultimately shooting himself dead on a subway platform. Brinsley also shot and wounded his ex-girlfriend before boarding a bus that morning from Baltimore to New York City. His attack on the officers was reportedly motivated by the rash of police killings of unarmed black people nationwide. Coincidentally, while Brinsley was carrying out his attack, poets were gathered in New York's Washington Square Park to read poems in protest of said killings."

Born in 1991, HIEU MINH NGUYEN is a queer Vietnamese American poet from St. Paul, Minnesota. He is the author of *This Way to the Sugar* (Write Bloody Press, 2014) and *Not Here* (Coffee House Press, 2018). Hieu is a 2018 McKnight Writing Fellow, a Kundiman Fellow, and a 2017 National Endowment for the Arts Literature Fellow. He is a graduate of the MFA Program for Writers at Warren Wilson College and is currently a Wallace Stegner Fellow at Stanford University.

SHARON OLDS was born in San Francisco in 1942 and educated at Stanford University and Columbia University. The winner of both the Pulitzer Prize and England's T. S. Eliot Prize for her 2012 collection, *Stag's Leap*, she is the author of ten previous books of poetry and the winner of many other awards and honors. Her latest books are *Odes* (2016) and *Arias* (2019), both from Alfred A. Knopf. Olds teaches in the Graduate Program of Creative Writing at New York University and helped to found the NYU workshop program for residents of

Goldwater Hospital on Roosevelt Island, and for veterans of Iraq and Afghanistan. She lives in New York City.

Of "Hyacinth Aria," Olds writes: "I think of myself as a poet without 'ideas' (whatever they are!—'Saturday is a day of the week'—is that an idea?). Rather I am a poet with stories, which often seem to arise in the presence of something seen, often something in the natural world. (Yes, I'm a narrative poet (sigh)—but a pagan narrative poet!)

"And when this most welcome invitation came, at first I had 'Amaryllis Ode' mixed up in my mind with 'Hyacinth Aria.' (And there's another poem by me somewhere that refers to the hyacinth being called after Apollo's lament ('*Aiee!*' for his—fallen soldiers?).)

"Both poems had their beginnings in gazing at flowers—this one, looking at bulbs in water, seeing the sexual floral, feeling moved, then the leap back from the speaker's adult (late) mother to the mother as child, seen as a backyard faerie something like a damselfly, then tracing a Sin of abuse back toward some Original practitioner.

"And I've been trying harder—especially since 2006–2014, my years with Carl in New Hampshire—to be more truthful and accurate in poems. Thus 'for a moment, / I love my mother,' and the last line's first half, which was added to the poem an hour later—as if, if one just hates one's parents, has *no* love for them, how hard it would be to become fully human, or a good citizen."

MATTHEW OLZMANN was born in Detroit, Michigan, in 1976. He is the author of two collections of poems, *Mezzanines* (2013) and *Contradictions in the Design* (2016), both from Alice James Books. His third book of poems, *Constellation Route*, is forthcoming in January 2022. He teaches at Dartmouth College and in the MFA Program for Writers at Warren Wilson College.

Of "Letter to the Person Who, During the Q&A Session After the Reading, Asked for Career Advice," Olzmann writes: "As the title suggests, this poem began as a response to a type of question that I imagine many authors receive during a post-reading Q&A. It's a type of question that I love, and one that reminds me of when I was in the early stages of trying to imagine a way to become a writer. I used to go to readings, concerts, and art openings and be in absolute awe of these artists doing these things that seemed quite mysterious and impossible. Even now, art has that effect on me; it still seems strange and astonishing, though I might now be slightly better equipped to put that feeling into words. I remember sitting in the audience back then thinking,

'How does that even happen? How do people do this?' by which I meant 'How can *I* do this?' This poem begins with that type of yearning in mind, and while it responds to a question from someone with a similar inquisitive spirit, I also see it as an actual letter to that earlier incarnation of myself, someone full of hope and amazement, trying to find a path into and through some great mystery."

Born and raised in St. Paul, Minnesota, PAUL OTREMBA is the author of *Levee* (2019), *Pax Americana* (2015), and *The Currency* (2009), all from Four Way Books. He taught at Rice University and in the Warren Wilson College MFA Program for Writers. He studied English and philosophy at the University of Minnesota before receiving a Master of Fine Arts degree from the University of Maryland and a doctorate in creative writing and literature from the University of Houston. He taught at Southern Methodist University in Dallas, driving home to Houston every weekend, before arriving at Rice University in 2012. "Living in Houston for the past fourteen years, I have gone through three major hurricanes and two devastating floods," Otremba told Rick Barot, the poetry editor of *New England Review* in 2018. "I'm also thinking about contemporary ecopoetics with what Timothy Morton, my brilliant colleague at Rice, calls hyperobjects, or things massively distributed in space and time that challenge our attempts to wholly grasp them, things such as global warming, Styrofoam, microbeads of plastic, fossil fuels." Paul Otremba died from stomach cancer, at the age of forty, in 2019.

CECILY PARKS was born in New York in 1976. She is the author of the poetry collections *Field Folly Snow* (University of Georgia, 2008) and *O'Nights* (Alice James, 2015) and the editor of *The Echoing Green: Poems of Fields, Meadows, and Grasses* (Everyman's Library, 2016). She teaches in the MFA program at Texas State University.

Parks writes: " 'The Seeds' is the longest poem I've written to date. The poem came about, in part, from looking up the word 'hope' in a dictionary. In its secondary definitions, hope can refer to a parcel of protected land or a cove of calm water. Thinking about hope as a landscape helped me to give shape to the feeling of hope as I've felt it over the past decade."

CARL PHILLIPS was born in Everett, Washington, in 1959. His most recent collections of poetry are *Pale Colors in a Tall Field* (Farrar, Straus and Giroux, 2020) and the chapbook *Star Map with Action Figures* (Sibling Rivalry, 2019). Phillips teaches at Washington University in St. Louis.

Of "Something to Believe In," Phillips writes: "I only have one hunting dog—not two—but as I lay in bed one night, listening to the breathing of the dog to one side of me, my partner on the other side, and my own breathing, I fell into a dream about which I remembered nothing upon waking except this poem's opening sentence and its last two sentences. This has never happened to me before. I immediately grabbed my phone and typed the lines into the notes, then wrote the poem the next morning. I suppose it concerns assumptions and complacency, about our fellow animals and humans, about domesticity and violence, about certainty and instability when it comes to history. The occasional recognition that we are all animals, and anything could happen at any time. . . ."

STANLEY PLUMLY was born in Barnseville, Ohio, in 1939 and died in April of 2019. He was Distinguished University Professor of English at the University of Maryland. His eleven books of poetry include *Old Heart*, winner of the *Los Angeles Times* Book Prize in 2008, and a posthumous volume, *Middle Distance* (W. W. Norton, 2020). He also published four books of prose on poetics and English Romantic poets. He wrote with great fervor about John Keats, "the eternally young autumnal poet," and his great ode "To Autumn" as an instance of what Keats called "negative capability." Keats's "impersonal" ideal was, according to Plumly, "what most distances him from the narrative impulse in Wordsworth and the conversation poems of Coleridge, and what distinguishes him from the didacticism of Shelley."

JANA PRIKRYL was born in Ostrava, Czechoslovakia, in 1975. Her family fled the country in 1980 and eventually immigrated to Canada, where she grew up. She is the author of two books of poems, *No Matter* (2019) and *The After Party* (2016), both published by Tim Duggan Books. Her essays can be found mainly in *The Nation* and *The New York Review of Books*, where she is a senior editor and the poetry editor. *No Matter* was written thanks to a 2017–2018 fellowship at the Radcliffe Institute for Advanced Study at Harvard University.

Of "Fox," Prikryl writes: "This poem grew out of a flash of memory, from when I was around four years old and lived in Czechoslovakia. That was sometime before my family fled to Austria and eventually Canada; the initial memory in the poem glimpses my parents' argument over whether we ought to leave. Somehow the lines needed to be short, the diction telegraphic, couplets studding the text with additional interruptions or hesitations. I hesitate to say any more; this much already borders on falsification!"

KEVIN PRUFER, born in 1969 in Cleveland, Ohio, is the author of several collections of poetry, most recently *How He Loved Them* (2018), *Churches* (2014), and *In a Beautiful Country* (2011), all from Four Way Books. He also cocurates the Unsung Masters Series, which brings the work of little-known, out-of-print authors to new readers. He teaches at the University of Houston's creative writing program and at Lesley University's low-residency MFA program.

Of "Archaeology," Prufer writes: "I've always preferred *not* writing about myself, comfortable with the idea that the world of the not-me is wider and more interesting than my own experience. But this poem is different. My father was an archaeologist and he kept human remains in the basement, where he'd made a makeshift office away from the university. I was fascinated by the skulls, especially one with a quarter-size hole in the forehead. A fatal wound, he called it. Of course, this was deeply problematic, though as a boy I didn't understand that. They were just wonderful, sinister objects to me. I was looking at a photo of him against a backdrop of human skulls when I wrote this poem."

ARIANA REINES was born in Salem, Massachusetts. She is the author of four books of poetry and the Obie-winning play *Telephone*. *A Sand Book* (Tin House, 2019) won the 2020 Kingsley Tufts Poetry Award.

Of "A Partial History," Reines writes: "This poem came out in one go. I wrote it in the T. S. Eliot house in Gloucester. I think the dead poet helped me write it, with everything that was wrong with him and with everything that was right with him."

MAX RITVO was born in 1990 and died in 2016 not yet having reached his twenty-sixth birthday. He wrote his first book, *Four Reincarnations*, in New York and Los Angeles during a long battle with cancer. His subsequent books, *The Final Voicemails*, edited by Louise Glück, and *Letters from Max,* coauthored by Sarah Ruhl, were both published posthumously. All three books were published by Milkweed Editions. Ritvo's poetry also appeared in *The New Yorker* and *Poetry* among other publications.

In an email interview with Justin Boening (*Literary Hub*, September 7, 2016), Ritvo has this riff on why death is "hilarious." He gives a few reasons (the "physical comedy," for one) and then "death is also hilarious because uncomfortably long silences are hilarious. Andy Kaufman, Tim Heidecker, there are genius comedians whose entire careers are built on uncomfortable silences that resolve in underwhelming utterances. And death is the longest and most uncomfortable silence in existence. And it resolves in the most underwhelming utterance—even more silence. And the dying person imposes it on every single person they've ever known. Your loved ones think about dead you even when you're not around—they think about you for decades, for their whole *lives* if you loved them enough. Death gives you an audience for your uncomfortable silence that has no geographic or temporal constraint. It gives you a forever stage (at least until your audience goes extinct)." When he is asked to characterize the relationship between entertainment and art, Ritvo says "the short answer is I've had a very hard life, and I think everyone, me included, deserves a break. I want my writing to heal people. And not like chemotherapy, but like a good veggie soup. Poetry must entertain if it is to heal."

CLARE ROSSINI was born in St. Paul, Minnesota. Her third collection, *Lingo* (2006), was published by University of Akron Press. *The Poetry of Capital*, an anthology she coedited, was published in 2020. Rossini is artist-in-residence in the English department at Trinity College in Hartford, Connecticut, teaching creative writing and directing an outreach program that places college students in inner-city public school arts classrooms.

Of "The Keeper Will Enter the Cage," Rossini writes: "One morning, I drifted awake seeing a man with his head in the mouth of a lion. That's one way to begin the day! I'd been working on a manuscript that weaves together poems about my brother's early death—a local grief—with poems addressing the vaster, more diffused, and ongoing losses brought on by climate change. The climate poems got me to thinking about where and how our relationship with nature went so wrong. Then came that morning dream-image, a suggestion, a gift.

"A book on the history of American circuses got me to Isaac A. Van Amburgh, the nineteenth-century 'Lion King,' who claimed to be the first man to put his head in the mouth of a lion. To make the act, Van Amburgh had to crush the lion's instinctive reactions, its spirit. I was interested in what sort of person has such ambitions. And more, whether he had to destroy something in himself, too: the innate human respect for the power and strangeness of wild animals, their intelligence and will.

"Van Amburgh's skill made him an international celebrity; he toured all the European capitals. When I read that Victoria, Matriarch of Empire, saw his act six times, I knew I had to get her into the poem. Perhaps Victoria saw Van Amburgh as a kindred spirit, his success proof of what could be gained by subjugating the natural world—a world that included, in Victoria's mind, the non-English peoples of the colonies. But aren't we all—Westerners, particularly—tamers of things natural? Good things have come from it, too. But also climate change, and the wildfires, droughts, and floods that accompany it, threatening every being that shares the planet.

"—But that brocade! Queen Victoria had a fondness for South Sea pearls, shipped back from the Empire's fisheries in India and Sri Lanka. And the necklace? A gift from Prince Albert, made with the teeth of a stag he'd killed during his first hunt. Just the thing for an outing to the circus."

ROBYN SCHIFF was born in 1973 and raised in New Jersey. She is the author of three poetry collections, *Worth* (2002), *Revolver* (2008), and most recently, *A Woman of Property* (2016), which was a finalist for the *Los Angeles Times* Book Prize. Schiff is a professor at Emory University in Atlanta, and coeditor of Canarium Books, a small press devoted to poetry.

Schiff writes: "'American Cockroach' was the first poem I wrote after the disgusting and inevitable presidential election of 2016. Since then, in the tradition of the epic, the poem has come to serve as the invocation of my forthcoming book-length poem, *Information Desk: An Epic*. In our corrupt age of spin, truthiness, and outright lies, I require a goddess of accuracy to protect me in my epic endeavor. With her double stinger evolved for neurosurgical precision, I invoke the Jewel Wasp as my muse."

BRANDON SOM was born in Phoenix, Arizona, in 1975. He is the author of *The Tribute Horse* (Nightboat Books), winner of the 2015 Kate Tufts Discovery Award, and the chapbook *Babel's Moon* (Tupelo Press). He currently lives in San Diego where he teaches in the literature department at UCSD.

Of "Shainadas," Som writes: "My maternal grandfather Ted

Mendoza was born during the Depression. As a result of seeing so many lose everything, he held on to everything. He kept his shoeshine box beneath the bed. I was always fascinated by it as an object. The box acts as a kind of time machine in the poem allowing me to look backward while the stanzas work their own optics of time and projection: the frame rate of images passing—cut with enjambment—on the film reel of the poetic line. But since my grandparents first met in a movie theater—the old Azteca, in downtown Phoenix—in which my maternal grandmother Pastora Mendoza worked concession and would eventually usher her future husband—looking at that shinebox was also projecting forward, seeing into their future."

JON WILLIAM STOUT was born in Denver, Colorado, in 1988. He attended Pacific Lutheran University and the Iowa Writers' Workshop. His poems have appeared in *New England Review*, *Lana Turner Journal*, and *Prelude*.

Of "Dysphonia," Stout writes: "This poem was a reconciliatory act I don't feel responsible for but lucky to have been caught by. Seeing my father's suffering, the incremental evidence of deterioration—how he tracked it, how he tracked me tracking it—while witnessing, too, his graceful engagement with it, I had to acknowledge resentments I held about pain from the past. We both love language. Epidemiological & pathophysiological terms interspersed throughout the poem are masks for a collaborative dance where we're both on stage & he's dying. The stage or setting draws on details from his apartment in Aurora, Colorado; they're banal; they reek. But their banality is the living that sees the specter of death in the distance, slow, foggy, the outcome certain; such details (thrushes, lilac, tomatoes, walking the dog, pot roast, hockey on TV) counterpoint the odd ekstasis of medical words; they brought us to our seats in his apartment, talking about something while the hockey is on."

ARTHUR SZE was born in New York City in 1950. His tenth book of poems, *Sight Lines* (Copper Canyon, 2019), won the 2019 National Book Award for Poetry. He is a professor emeritus at the Institute of American Indian Arts.

Sze writes: "This suite of nine poems is named 'Sprang' for (1) the past tense of 'to spring,' with its many meanings, and also for (2) its meaning as a hand-weaving technique in which threads or cords are intertwined and twisted over one another to form an openwork mesh. The loosely interwoven poems form a 'sprang of space and time' and include poems in memory of C. D. Wright and Eva Saulitis. Section #4, 'Kintsugi,' means 'golden repair' in Japanese. In traditional Japanese culture, when a ceramic pot is broken, the shards are reassembled and bound together with gold-dusted lacquer. This 'golden repair' does not disguise but highlights the breakage, and in writing this section, I conceived of silence as my gold lacquer."

Born in Kansas City, Missouri, in 1943, JAMES TATE (1943–2015) won the Yale Series of Younger Poets award for his book *The Lost Pilot* when he was twenty-three and still a student in the Iowa writing program. He became one of our most celebrated and innovative poets. In the history of the prose poem he is acknowledged as a major figure. He wrote a score of poetry books. *Selected Poems* (Wesleyan University Press, 1991) won him the Pulitzer; *Worshipful Company of Fletchers* (Ecco Press, 1994) earned him the National Book Award. *The Route as Briefed*, his prose book, is an eclectic collection that blends fiction, essays and interviews, and a long piece about the father he never met, killed in action during World War II, who was the "lost pilot" of the poet's first book. Tate wrote with a kind of deadpan surrealism that seemed to come naturally to him when he sat in front of a typewriter. He was very funny—his humor an aspect of his unique vision.

Tate, whose work has appeared in many volumes of *The Best American Poetry*, was the guest editor of our 1997 edition, in the introduction of which he wrote "In my experience poets are not different from other people. You have your dullards, your maniacs, your mild eccentrics, etc. Except for this one thing they do—write poems. And in this they are singularly strange. They may end up with an audience and a following of some sort, but in truth they write their poems with various degrees of obsessiveness mostly for themselves, for the pleasure and satisfaction it gives them. And for the hunger and need nothing else can abate."

Tate taught at the University of Massachusetts in Amherst, where he had a dedicated following, and lived in Pelham, Massachusetts. His posthumous book, *The Government Lake*, was released in July 2019 from Ecco/HarperCollins, followed by a paper edition in 2020. He died in 2015. He was married to the poet Dara Wier.

Born in 1974 in Athens, Georgia, BRIAN TEARE is the author of six books, most recently *Companion Grasses*, *The Empty Form Goes All the Way to Heaven*, and *Doomstead Days*. He has received the Brittingham

Prize and Lambda Literary and Publishing Triangle Awards, as well as fellowships from the NEA, the Pew Foundation, and the MacDowell Colony. An associate professor at the University of Virginia, he lives in Charlottesville, where he makes books by hand for his micropress, Albion Books.

Of "Sitting Isohydric Meditation," Teare writes: "How to keep going into an era of ever-deepening climate crisis? How to keep going into an age of ever-increasing physical degeneration? This poem asks both questions at once. When I lived in South Philadelphia, the street tree in its four-by-four plot outside the row home I rented was the only living thing I could see from inside. I grew very attached to it. In summer, the neighborhood's particularly hot because there are so few trees among the low brick homes that cast little shade; all the exposed city surfaces soak up sunlight and stay radiant late into the night. In that urban heat island, drought and extreme heat hit hard. The maple—I could never quite identify what kind presided over my stoop, though I admired its hot pink achenes each spring—is an isohydric tree, which means it closes its stomata to prevent losing water and attempts to wait out drought by surviving off stored sugars. During the drought summer of 2017, I underwent several MRIs to help diagnose the cause of restricted mobility and chronic pain. While I learned more about osteoarthritic spinal degeneration and what it *might* mean for my future, I spent more time on the couch, looking out at the maple whose leaves were beginning to brown. The challenge of suffering is to remain open to it; it is also the challenge of true intimacy. At some point that drought summer I realized I couldn't meet either challenge."

CRAIG MORGAN TEICHER was born in 1979. His books include *The Trembling Answers*, which won the 2017 Lenore Marshall Poetry Prize from the Academy of American Poets. He edited *Once and For All: The Best of Delmore Schwartz*, and is the author of the essay collection *We Begin in Gladness: How Poets Progress*.

Teicher writes: " 'I Am a Father Now' is a late-breaking installment in a series of 'I Am' poems that I initiated in my first book, *Brenda Is in the Room and Other Poems*, published way back in 2007. If that book was a record of the excitement and ambivalence, the giddy fear, of falling in love and leaning toward marriage, the book I am working on now, in which this poem appears, is about the surprise of finding oneself suddenly in middle age with two children, a family hamster, a mortgage, and a hell of a lot of bewildering responsibility. Utterly banal and rigged with all sorts of trip wires and booby traps, parenthood has accounted for much of the high drama in my life—everything shifts inside one's head, sort of behind one's back, in much the same way that the passage of time takes one by surprise. Finally, it *is* exciting, if one is willing to be thrilled by becoming the kind of grownup one spent decades fleeing. All of the poems in the series feature a few common elements—horses, bending down, a certain elevated sense of self-importance—and it was fun, more than a decade later, to find ways of incorporating all of them into a new setting. Things are always changing and they stay the same as they change, and poetry is the right place to articulate such silly paradoxes."

LYNNE THOMPSON was born in Los Angeles, California, in 1951. She is the author of three collections of poetry: *Beg No Pardon*, winner of the 2007 Perugia Press Prize, *Start with a Small Guitar* (What Books Press), and *Fretwork*, selected by Jane Hirshfield for the 2018 Marsh Hawk Press Poetry Prize. She has received an individual artist fellowship from the City of Los Angeles.

Of "She talk like this 'cause me Mum born elsewhere, say," Thompson writes: "I knew from a young age that my parents had come to America from small islands in the Caribbean. When they told me stories of the country of their birth, I concentrated on the details not the accent they wound around their stories. As I became more aware of the intonations of others, I began to understand that my parents' English was 'accented'; that is, they gave 'prominence to each syllable by stress or pitch' (*Oxford Pocket American Dictionary*) in ways that highlighted their status as immigrants. The poem is an homage to my mother's unique pronunciations and homegrown references, her way of speaking that makes its way into my own communications from time to time.

"I've always been intrigued by poems that employ an abecedarian form and thought it was the perfect vehicle for conveying my mother's struggle with language and pronunciation. The abecedarian allowed specific words to be highlighted in a way that might have been lost on the reader had the poem sought refuge in some other formal structure."

MATTHEW THORBURN was born in Lansing, Michigan, in 1973. He is the author of seven collections of poetry, including *The Grace of Distance* (Louisiana State University Press, 2019), the book-length poem *Dear Almost* (LSU Press, 2016) and the chapbook *A Green River in*

Spring (Autumn House Press, 2015). His work has been recognized with the Lascaux Prize in Collected Poetry, a Witter Bynner Fellowship from the Library of Congress, and fellowships from the Bronx and New Jersey arts councils and the Sewanee Writers' Conference. He works in corporate communications in New York City and lives near Princeton, New Jersey, with his wife and son.

Thorburn writes: "'The Stag' is part of a book-length sequence of poems about a teenage boy's experiences during a war and its aftermath. The boy loses his family, friends, and the girl he loves, but he lives to tell his story. As I tried to imagine my way into his head—What would it be like to lose so much? Could *I* keep going? Would I even want to?—I remembered a painting of a deer caught in a dense wood. While the branches are sharply outlined, Gerhard Richter's stag is blurred, as if about to disappear. I first saw the painting nearly twenty years ago in a retrospective of Richter's work at the Museum of Modern Art. This image stayed with me a long time before I found the right place for it in a poem."

MEHRNOOSH TORBATNEJAD was born in New York in 1986. Her poetry has appeared in NASA's short film *First Light*, the *Asian American Writers' Workshop*, and the *New England Review*, among others. She is the former poetry editor for *Noble / Gas Qtrly*, and winner of the 2019 *LUMINA* La Lengua contest and the 2016 *Pinch* Literary Prize. She lives in New York where she practices law.

Of "Isfahan, 2010," Torbatnejad writes: "I wrote this poem after returning to New York from a visit to Iran, when I suddenly realized how alienating it feels to accept the continuous mispronunciation of my name. You don't take a break from your name, so the expectation that I have to repeat mine can be laborious. That everyone in Iran pronounced it like it was just any other name was extraordinary. And I especially loved the small breath they took when they spoke the first H in my name; a letter that is often skipped when mispronounced."

COREY VAN LANDINGHAM was born in Ashland, Oregon, in 1986. She is the author of *Antidote* (The Ohio State University Press, 2013) and *Love Letter to Who Owns the Heavens*, forthcoming from Tupelo Press. A recipient of a National Endowment for the Arts Fellowship and a Wallace Stegner Fellowship from Stanford University, she teaches in the MFA program at the University of Illinois.

Of "Recessional," Van Landingham writes: "Poetry is, for me, ultimately a form of proximity. It both acknowledges and closes distances. Love poems, which create a sense of intimacy and seek to bridge a distance between lover and beloved, writer and reader, rely on aesthetic distance to fashion these illusions. And if distance is what allows for love and beauty and poetry, then it, too, allows—as drone strikes remind us—the objectification of the other. The 'you' in a love poem is always more and less than reality. So, too, the body on a screen. It is this remove—the anaesthetizing and dehumanizing distance from the drone to its target—that I find utterly terrifying. I am trying, then, to write poems that call attention to distance in its many forms, to write about love and violence in a way that makes the body concrete, unavoidable, dangerous."

ROSANNA WARREN was born in 1953 in Fairfield, Connecticut. She has published five books of poems, and various translations and works of literary criticism. *De notre vivant*, her selected poems in French translation by Aude Pivin, came out in France in 2019. Her biography of the French poet Max Jacob will be published by W. W. Norton in 2020.

Of "Samson, 1674," Warren writes: "The poem was originally a commission from the Milton Society of America. I have loved Milton's poetry since my adolescence, and occult allusions to him are threaded through my work. But since 2016, he has been in my mind more intensely than ever, as a political force of conscience, and resistance to tyranny. He's a poet (and prose writer) in whom the political and the literary imagination fuse to the utmost degree. A rare case."

ROBERT WRIGLEY lives with his wife, the writer Kim Barnes, in the woods near Moscow, Idaho. His most recent books are *Box* (Penguin, 2017) and *Anatomy of Melancholy & Other Poems* (Penguin, 2013).

Of "Machinery," Wrigley writes: "I might have been twelve or thirteen when my father explained to me the function of the dead-blow hammer. I soon forgot what such a hammer (or, as my father called it, a 'beatin' machine') was used for, but I never lost the name. Over his long life, my father accumulated and used thousands of tools. He was exceptionally skillful with them, building, repairing, and improving all sorts of things. If he did not quite understand the things I made or the tools with which I made them, he understood the importance of making as a fundamental human activity. As for the vocabulary that came with his tools and the work he did with them, it is now part of my own."

RYO YAMAGUCHI, born in 1981 on Guam, is the author of *The Refusal of Suitors* (2015), published by Noemi Press. Currently traveling full-time, he was most recently based in Seattle as the publicity and marketing director for Wave Books. Please visit him at plotsandoaths .com.

Yamaguchi writes: "I am often challenged in my reading life by distraction and an inability to concentrate—in part because so much of my reading takes place on commutes and in public settings, such as the beach in 'Reading Not Reading,' which is at Carkeek Park in north Seattle, close to where we lived. It's frustrating to have intrusions on your reading, but as I've aged I've also come to enjoy its effects, how the permeable boundaries between the book, your imagination, memories, and the external environment can allow for meaningfully layered mental activities and impressions. (Falling asleep reading—and then dreaming of that reading—is another wonderful example.) This layering can extend outward into social realms—for example, when you are reading alongside someone else, such as a longtime partner, maybe occasionally sharing your reading with each other. (Even as I type this, my wife is telling me about a news article she is reading.) I find this casual leisure reading can often lead to a rich blurring of consciousness and concerns, memories and hopes, and engender an urgency in wanting to express the inchoate understandings toward which such synthesis compel you. This poem wrestles with that urgency, a striving toward connection of important private experiences with a loved one."

JOHN YAU was born in Lynn, Massachusetts, in 1950. He is the author of seventeen books of poetry and fiction and numerous monographs on contemporary art. His most recent book of poetry is *Bijoux in the Dark* (Letter Machine Editions, 2018). Omindawn will publish his next of poetry, *Genghis Chan on Drums*, in fall 2021. In 2018, he was awarded the Jackson Poetry Prize, which is awarded annually by Poets & Writers to "an American poet of exceptional talent who deserves wider recognition." He lives in New York.

Of "The President's Telegram," Yau writes: "The poem was written in answer to the president's posting on his Twitter account after a former student shot and killed seventeen students and wounded seventeen others at Marjory Stoneman Douglas High School in Parkland, Florida, on February 14, 2008. It uses only the words that the president used in his Twitter condolences."

EMILY YONG was born in Hong Kong in 1955 and grew up in Brooklyn, New York. She graduated from Yale University (1977) with a BA, cum laude, in philosophy. She was the Rona Jaffe Poetry Scholar at Bread Loaf Writers' Conference in 2015. She lives in the Silicon Valley, where she is a practicing physician in internal medicine, and is working on her first collection of poems.

Of "Opioid, Alcohol, Despair," Yong writes: "My first patient, when I was an intern on duty, in 1982, bled out from varices from the esophagus. I remembered the ferocity of the hands of our ICU team to save him, that night, from annihilation. We failed. He was nineteen and had started drinking at age nine. I never once saw his face under all those tubes. Through the years, the danger of the body given over to addiction has been, though not as dramatic, ever present. The tremoring in the muscles in the hand, the leg. The inflammation in the liver, the brain. 'Insults' to organs, we called them, before the ship sank. The stroke. Cancer of the throat. In former days it was mostly alcohol; there were drugs, too, 'narcotics,' cocaine. Despite my sincere efforts to get my patients to stay sober, it was a constant roller-coaster ride of mixed feelings: defeat—anger, even—every time they relapsed, after a fourth round of rehab. It was a quandary for us who labored in the profession to help others who 'couldn't help themselves.' Mostly I left it to my trusted colleagues to deal with the mind's workings—the 'behavior' medicine specialists, the mental health care providers, social workers—who felt just as beleaguered as I. We were just learning to use PET scans/MRI on the brain. 'Substance use disorder' was starting to be defined, redefined—twenty years apart!—in between the fourth and fifth *DSM* revisions. Now of course we know it as the opioid 'crisis.'

"When I started writing ten years ago, the last thing I wanted was to write about those pent-up feelings of ambivalence, frustration—above all, the feelings of hopelessness, helplessness, sadness—in all of this. I wanted to write about flowers, the evening sky. The day after I saw the documentary (one reviewer called it 'a tragic masterpiece') of Amy Winehouse—found dead at home, age twenty-eight—I knew I wanted to write about it. Not so much to paint Munch's *Scream* but Van Gogh's *Starry Night*. Winehouse's famous lyrics *They tried to make me go to rehab but I said no, no, no* resounded in my brain; touched me. Not just her, but all the others (Hendrix, Joplin, Whitney, oh, you know their names)—not 'patients'—these larger-than-life stars in our universe. And the countless homeless nameless . . .

"And where do I begin—this—*love story*? The form of the poem helped me to constrain my mix of feelings. For the title, I kept the enormity—'Opioid, Alcohol, Despair'—in all its abstraction and universality that recognizes no economic/social bounds. The rest of the poem: how to bring the abstraction down a few notches? This would be a eulogy, after all. Would the hero be the addict? Briefly, I considered him as the speaker, but I knew such a first-person voice could not ring true, no matter how fictitiously-*real* I tried to conjure him. The only way for me was to experience him through the speaker of the poem, as she grapples—discovers—through the process of the writing, her conflicted feelings. The poem begins with the speaker almost addressing this person directly: *Feel for your lying there* . . . and immediately, and for the rest of the poem, switches to the third-person *he/him*. The poem remains an effort to engage with someone whom the speaker will not likely address in the second person again. At least not where she's out walking, out of her comfort zone—outside the hospital, not wearing her white coat. It is a poem just as much about the speaker struggling to *take notice* of those whom she's resisted noticing—the 'abstraction'— in the street. In the bleak landscape that is the world without the hospital lights—she sees and not sees. Ultimately the poem is about this gaze. *Is* that gaze. I hope through the language of the poem, the reader experiences with the speaker, if only just a bit, the sufferings and vulnerabilities of the body and the mind (which are inseparable) of those afflicted by addiction. Let poetry take them out of the shadow. This is the first step, of *seeing*, of connection. Understanding. Repair. A bit of tenderness—hope."

MONICA YOUN was born in Berkeley, California, in 1971 and was raised in Houston, Texas, the daughter of Korean immigrants. A former lawyer, she is the author of three books of poems, most recently *Blackacre* (Graywolf Press, 2016), which was named one of the best poetry books of the year by the *New York Times*, the *Washington Post* and *BuzzFeed*. She has been awarded the Williams Carlos Williams Award of the Poetry Society of America and the Levinson Prize from the Poetry Foundation. She has also been awarded a Guggenheim Fellowship, the Library of Congress/Witter Bynner Fellowship, and a fellowship from Stanford University. She teaches creative writing at Princeton University and in the MFA programs at Columbia University and NYU.

Of "Study of Two Figures (Pasiphaë/Sado)," Youn writes: "Some background information might be helpful here. In classical Greek mythology, Pasiphaë was the wife of King Minos of Crete. She was from

Colchis, in modern-day Turkey, from the same family as Circe, Medea, and Phaedra. The gods sent Minos a white bull from the sea, which Minos was supposed to sacrifice to the gods. Instead Minos kept the bull for his own herds, and as a punishment, the gods made Pasiphaë fall in love with the bull. She instructed the inventor Daedalus to fabricate a hollow wooden cow and she hid inside the cow in order to have sex with the bull. She was impregnated by the bull and gave birth to the Minotaur, which was imprisoned in the Labyrinth until it was killed by the hero Theseus. In Korean history Crown Prince Sado (originally named Jangheon) was an eighteenth-century prince and the heir to the throne. He married, and had a son who would be third in line for the throne. He later developed a homicidal mania, in which he killed and raped many courtiers. His father, King Yeongjo, faced a dilemma: The king could not kill Sado because the body of a royal was sacrosanct, and he could not condemn Sado as a criminal because Sado's son, the only remaining male heir, would also share in his father's condemnation and punishment. On a hot July day, the king ordered Sado to appear before him, to apologize for his crimes, and to climb into a wooden rice chest (approximately 4×4×4). Sado obeyed. The king ordered the rice chest to be tied shut and covered with grass. After eight days in the rice chest, Sado died."

MATTHEW ZAPRUDER was born in Washington, D.C., in 1967. He is the author of five collections of poetry, most recently *Father's Day*, from Copper Canyon in 2019, as well as *Why Poetry*, a book of prose. He is editor at large at Wave Books, and teaches in the MFA program at Saint Mary's College of California.

Zapruder writes: "I wrote 'My Life' in the summer of 2018 as part of a daily practice of writing poems back and forth with my friend Matt Rohrer. At the time, I thought they were only between us, a private correspondence. This allowed me to say many things I might not otherwise, using whatever poetic techniques were required in order to discover the truth, or at least the essential questions. In this case I began to address not Matt, but my wife. I suppose it was my own version of Frank O'Hara's deadly unserious manifesto 'Personism,' in which he discovers a way of writing poems in which you realize you can 'use the telephone instead of writing the poem' but choose to write the poem anyway, and thus a movement is born. O'Hara writes, 'In all modesty, I confess that it may be the death of literature as we know it. . . . Poetry being quicker and surer than prose, it is only just that poetry finish literature off.' "

Academy of American Poets Poem-a-Day, guest eds. Clint Smith (February), Maggie Smith (March), and Paul Guest (July). www.poets
.org

The Adroit Journal, poetry eds. Emily Cinquemani, Kate Gaskin, Wayne Johns, and Talin Tahajian. www.theadroitjournal.org

AGNI, poetry eds. Jennifer Kwon Dobbs and Ruben Quesada. www
.agnionline.bu.edu

The American Poetry Review, ed. Elizabeth Scanlon. www.aprweb.org

The Asian American Literary Review, editors-in-chief Lawrence-Minh Bùi Davis and Gerald Maa. www.aalrmag.org

Cave Wall, eds. Rhett Iseman Trull and Jeff Trull; official poem accepter Audrey Trull. www.cavewallpress.com

Cherry Tree, editor-in-chief and poetry ed. James Allen Hall. www
.washcoll.edu/centers/lithouse/cherry-tree/

The Cincinnati Review, poetry ed. Rebecca Lindenberg. www.cincinnati
review.com

The Commuter [Electric Literature], eds. Kelly Luce and Ed Skoog.
www.electricliterature.com/the-commuter

Conduit, editor-in-chief William D. Waltz. www.conduit.org

Copper Nickel, poetry eds. Brian Barker and Nicky Beer. www.copper
-nickel.org

Fence, ed. Rebecca Wolff; poetry eds. Tonya Foster, Paul Legault, Farid Matuk, Soham Patel, Charles Valle, and Max Winter. www.fence
portal.org

The Georgia Review, ed. Gerald Maa. www.thegeorgiareview.com

The Gettysburg Review, ed. Mark Drew. www.gettysburgreview.com

Harvard Review, poetry ed. Major Jackson. www.harvardreview.org

The Iowa Review, poetry ed. Abby Petersen. www.iowareview.org

jubilat, eds. Caryl Pagel and Emily Pettit. www.jubilat.org

Kenyon Review, poetry ed. David Baker. www.kenyonreview.org

Mānoa, ed. Frank Stewart. *www.manoa.hawaii.edu*

The Massachusetts Review, poetry eds. Ellen Doré Watson and Deborah Gorlin. www.massreview.org

Michigan Quarterly Review, ed. Khaled Mattawa. www.michiganquarterly review.com

Mississippi Review, editor-in-chief Adam Clay. www.mississippireview .com

The Nation, poetry eds. Stephanie Burt and Carmen Giménez Smith. www.thenation.com

New England Review, poetry ed. Rick Barot. www.nereview.com

New Ohio Review, ed. David Wanczyk, assistant poetry editor Lee Spellman. www.ohio.edu/nor

The New York Review of Books, poetry ed. Jana Prikryl. www.nybooks .com

The New Yorker, poetry ed. Kevin Young. www.newyorker.com

The Paris Review, poetry ed. Vijay Seshadri. www.theparisreview.org

Parnassus, ed. Herbert Leibowitz. www.parnassusreview.com

Pleiades, poetry eds. Jenny Molberg and Erin Adair-Hodges. www .pleiadesmag.org

Ploughshares, poetry ed. John Skoyles. www.pshares.org

Poetry, ed. Don Share. www.poetryfoundation.org

Poetry Daily, editorial director Sally Keith. www.poems.com

Poetry Northwest, ed. Keetje Kuipers. www.poetrynw.org

Poetry Society of America, "Poetry & Democracy" feature, ed. Brett Fletcher Lauer. www.poetrysociety.org

Prairie Schooner, editor-in-chief Kwame Dawes. www.prairieschooner .unl.edu

Salamander, poetry ed. Anna V. Q. Ross. www.salamandermag.org

The Sewanee Review, ed. Adam Ross. www.thesewaneereview.com

The Southern Review, poetry ed. Jessica Faust. www.thesouthernreview .org

Tin House, www.tinhouse.com

Virginia Quarterly Review, poetry ed. Gregory Pardlo. www.vqronline .org

Waxwing, poetry eds. W. Todd Kaneko and Justin Bigos. www.wax wingmag.org

ZYZZYVA, ed. Laura Cogan. www.zyzzyva.org

ACKNOWLEDGMENTS

The series editor thanks Mark Bibbins for his invaluable assistance. Warm thanks go also to Denise Duhamel, Amy Gerstler, Dana Gioia, Stacey Harwood, and Major Jackson; to Glen Hartley and Lynn Chu of Writers' Representatives; and to Kathy Belden, David Stanford Burr, Dan Cuddy, Erich Hobbing, and Rosie Mahorter at Scribner. The poetry editors of the magazines that were our sources deserve applause; they are the secret heroes of contemporary poetry.

Grateful acknowledgment is made of the magazines in which these poems first appeared and the magazine editors who selected them. A sincere attempt has been made to locate all copyright holders. Unless otherwise noted, copyright to the poems is held by the individual poets.

Julia Alvarez, "Saving the Children" from *The Nation*. Reprinted by permission of the poet.

Brandon Amico, "Customer Loyalty Program" from *Kenyon Review*. Reprinted by permission of the poet.

Rick Barot, "The Galleons" from *The Galleons*. © 2019 by Rick Barot. Reprinted by permission of Milkweed Editions. Also appeared in *Poetry*,

Kaveh Bassiri, "Invention of I" from *Copper Nickel*. Reprinted by permission of the poet.

Reginald Dwayne Betts, "A Man Drops a Coat on the Sidewalk and Almost Falls into the Arms of Another" from *Felon*. © 2019 by Reginald Dwayne Betts. Reprinted by permission of W. W. Norton, Inc. Also appeared in *Tin House*.

Ryan Black, "Nothing Beats a Fair" from *The Southern Review*. Reprinted by permission of the poet.

Bruce Bond, "Bells" from *Michigan Quarterly Review*. Reprinted by permission of the poet.

William Brewer, "Orange" from *The American Poetry Review*. Reprinted by permission of the poet.

Lucie Brock-Broido, "Tender" from *Parnassus*. Reprinted by permission of the Estate of Lucie Brock-Broido.